What an engaging read, splattered with gems which will make you think and think again about life, living, dying and what education, teaching and schools are, and how, at their best, they might excite and influence. Idiosyncratic it is, with its Thunks and its apparent kaleidoscopic randomness, but all the more worth reading because, or despite of, all that.

Christopher Day, Professor of Education, University of Nottingham

For 20 years Ian Gilbert's company Independent Thinking has encouraged us to think independently. Never has that been more important. His new book is a wonderful celebration of how education should be about more than value-added: it should be 'values-added'. Ian Gilbert exudes strong values and clear principles. His writing is endlessly inventive and refreshing, and his ideas serve as an uplifting antidote to an educational world which can too often feel dispiriting, mechanical and joyless. This is a book to read and keep returning to, to rejuvenate us in the darker days of term-time. Highly recommended.

Geoff Barton, Head Teacher, King Edward VI School, Suffolk

Ian Gilbert has provided us with a wonderful, entertaining smorgasbord of a read. The author offers insights into his personal history and charts the ways in which this has influenced his own intellectual development. In doing so, he continually challenges our assumptions and delivers some perceptive comments on current educational practice. Although the book differers from conventional educational offerings, readers will undoubtedly find themselves forced to rethink their ideas about the best way to prepare today's children for life in tomorrow's world.

Professor Maurice Galton, Faculty of Education, University of Cambridge

I enjoyed the latest book by my namesake – but not relative I should hasten to add!

Independent Thinking is a teacher-friendly book in many ways. First, for busy classroom teachers, like me, it can be dipped in and out of and you'll find treasure on every page: a pearl of wisdom to motivate you; a wonderful 'Thunk' to get you rethinking a subject with a fascinating question; a meditation upon the purpose of education to make you think about why you're teaching; an incisive observation about young people to enable you to see them in a different light; an autobiographical reflection to help you see how we're all connected by our common familial experiences; and points to help you be a better parent or professional.

Second, this book is informed by a philosophy which is both coherent and creative. A unifying theme permeates it, which is possibly encapsulated by one of Gilbert's aphorisms: 'Creativity starts with "If only …" Mediocrity ends with it.'

Francis Gilbert, author of *I'm A Teacher, Get Me Out Of Here*

In the modern world of education, it has become commonplace for individuals, groups and companies to offer solutions for our every need. Education, through its obsession with data, 'outstanding' lessons and results, has led to the need for silver bullets and quick-fix solutions. This is what makes Ian Gilbert's *Independent Thinking* such a refreshing book to read. Through an eclectic mix of stories, reflections and Thunks, the book fosters the very process which gives it its title. Reading this book will not provide any solutions but will act as fertile jump-off points to new questions and thinking as you engage with the many ideas explored here. There is a wide selection of topics, insights and perspectives but running through them is a strong Freirean philosophy and a belief in the goodness and potential of humanity.

This is a book which can be used in a number of different ways, from a starting point for personal reflection to a focus for collaborative discussion. One element which I find particularly positive is the lack of a simple, linear narrative; the reader can engage with as little or as much of the content as they wish, and can engage with the ideas in an order that suits them. Deleuze, the French philosopher, argues that we should think with the world rather than about it; this book, for me, embodies this ideal.

Dr Phil Wood, School of Education, University of Leicester

Independent Thinking is scattered with Ian Gilbert's own life experiences, using them to highlight his passion about what education should be. This is a must-read for teachers, parents, students, anyone with an interest in how our children are taught, and most importantly those responsible for designing and influencing the school curriculum!

From the first page to the last page, *Independent Thinking* is not only easy to read, but easy to relate to, easy to agree with almost everything written on every page, easy to say 'Yes, why isn't that happening?' and easy to write a list of all those you would like to read it. It isn't easy to put down and it won't be one of those books Ian describes in one of his bookshelf chapters, with the remark that 'if you have a book but don't read it within three months give it to someone else'.

Number 1 in the list of 42 uses for this book is 'To help you think' and it does just that. Using at times personal examples from throughout his life, he questions why 'thinking' is not integrated into teaching as naturally as it should be, which in turn makes the reader ask the same question. The arguments made for why it should be are hard to argue against.

Latifa Hassanali, Programme Manager,
'a prestigious international school near London'

Independent Thinking neutralises feedback by pointing out that it is an expression of the preferences, prejudices and limitations of the reviewer. That being so, I will confess to limitations of time and a preference for dipping in and out. Luckily 'dipping in and out' is one of the intended uses of this book.

I can have a lot of fun with a Thunk – 'Is never longer than forever?' or 'What are the achievements of a newborn baby?' are satisfying questions to ponder or discuss. I enjoy certainty, too. In my world, the answers to the Thunks 'Is it more important to do "I love you" than to say "I love you"?' and 'Can you be a head teacher if you've never been a teacher and can you be a good head teacher if you've never been a good teacher?' are 'Yes'. It's not lost on me that my certainty makes me an object of mistrust.

As to prejudices, what is the point of education? I know it isn't to replicate 'What works for me ...' Can the bogeyman that phrase conjures really be defeated by one little boy refusing to write his answers down? That, it seems to me, is the question at the heart of this book. Will it be used to start a revolution? Only if we use it to help us think. I did.

Rachael Wardell, Corporate Director,
Communities Directorate, West Berkshire Council

Independent Thinking

Ian Gilbert

Independent Thinking Press

First published by

Independent Thinking Press

Crown Buildings, Bancyfelin, Carmarthen, Wales, SA33 5ND, UK

www.independentthinkingpress.com

Independent Thinking Press is an imprint of Crown House Publishing Ltd.

© Ian Gilbert, 2014

The right of Ian Gilbert to be identified as the author of this work has been asserted by him in accordance with the Copyright, Designs and Patents Act 1988.

Illustration © Tania Willis, 2014.

Early versions of the following chapters first appeared in their original form on www.independentthinking.co.uk: pp. 15-17: 'A Ten-Step Parent Guide to Supporting Child's Learning in the Early Years'. pp. 105-107: 'How to Know Whether You're a Humanist or a Scientist'. pp. 148-150: '21 Ways of Knowing You Have Spent Too Long on Twitter'. pp. 163-167: 'The Intelligence of Six' Many of the Thunks™ and Twunks throughout the book have also appeared on Twitter @ThatIanGilbert. Quote page 24, under Crown Copyright.

Cover photograph © Gardner Hamilton www.gardnerhamilton.com

Cover illustration by Tania Willis www.taniawillis.com

British Library Cataloguing-in-Publication Data

A catalogue entry for this book is available from the British Library.

Print ISBN 978-178135055-3
Mobi ISBN 978-178135078-2
ePub ISBN 978-178135079-9
ePDF ISBN 978-178135080-5

Printed and bound in the UK by

Gomer Press, Llandysul, Ceredigion

To Mónica

For bringing me back to life

Contents

Do things no one does or do things everyone does in a way no one does

These Are My Thoughts
Get Your Own

I don't believe in systems. In pre-packaged answers to everyday questions. If you think about something long enough to come up with a response and then act on it then you have at least proven you exist, or rather made it worthwhile existing. Your response might be the same as everyone else's, but it is still your response and has more value than the off-the-shelf answers peddled by the people with something to sell and an army of shelf stackers.

I set up Independent Thinking in 1993 as an organisation to encourage young people to use their thoughts to get more out of their lives. I had no idea what it would look like or where it would take me. I still don't, 20 years later. It's a 'for-profit company' but was set up, I now realise, to make a difference, not to make a profit. If the only thing it has done in 20 years is to encourage more people to think for themselves – to reflect, to think, to think deeply, to think independently and then to act in a similar spirit – then it will have been worthwhile.

The journey, like most people's, has been a hard one. Everyone has their heartaches. Their baggage. Their story. While you cannot avoid misfortune it is particularly easy to avoid opportunity. Simply keep your head down being busy. It will soon pass on to someone else. The challenge is to create, spot and then seize the opportunities. Success isn't the goal – it's the process that counts. That way, every day is a success, no matter how hard it is. You can only do this, though, if you see life as an adventure. When you do it means that, no matter what happens, it is all simply 'part of the adventure'. It is not actually anything at all to do with that so-called 'real life' where you have to be serious and grown up. It's just an adventure. In fact, when nothing is real life, everything is OK.

It doesn't make for an easy life but it does make for an interesting one. You can have one or the other but you can't have both. You have to choose.

I was asked to write this book to capture the spirit of what independent thinking – not Independent Thinking – is all about. Which is a hard one. A book of my thoughts to encourage you to have thoughts of your own. The most I can do is to put down in print what I think and how I think in the hope that this will act as a stimulus to your own thinking. Some of the thoughts I have recorded here are short one-liners. Others are longer, but that is usually because I haven't had the time to make them shorter. Either way I hope the effect will be the same – to use my thoughts to stimulate your own.

And what is it I spend most of my time thinking about? Well, for over 20 years it has been about education, not only what goes on in the classroom but education in its wider sense of helping the world think. If there is one idea that has informed my thinking in recent years, it is one inspired by the great Brazilian educationalist Paolo Freire who worked with illiterate farm and plantation workers in Brazil and Chile in the 1960s and 1970s.[1] It is that the highest goal

1   P. Freire, *Pedagogy of Hope* (London: Continuum, 1992).

of education is to teach people to 'read and write the word' so they can come to 're-read and re-write the world'.

We spend a great deal of effort, in the developed world at least, on the former but we tend to overlook the latter. Yet if we teach young people that this is the way the world is and leave it there, we are supporting the status quo and making of them passive observers. The 'object' not the 'subject' of their world, as Freire would have it. To teach them, as part of the day-to-day process of educating them in a broad curriculum, that this is the way the world is currently and why that is the case, and to maintain a constant eye on helping them know that it doesn't always have to be that way, that such a state is transitory and they can work to bring to bear an influence that will make it different if they choose to – now that's what I call an education.

3

Through simple dialogue based on a position of humility, not of academic arrogance, Freire could help superstitious peasant workers move from a fatalistic stance of: 'You're better than I am because you're educated and I'm not and that's God's way' to: 'No, God isn't the cause of all this. It's the boss!'[2] He was imprisoned as a traitor and then exiled from Brazil after the military coup in 1964. Of course he was.

In recent years, after the death of my first wife and finding new happiness and perspectives with the lady to whom this book is dedicated, my thinking has been further fuelled by time spent in living in the Middle East, in Latin America and now in the Far East. Despite the fact that J. S. Bach never left Germany

2 Ibid.

and Immanuel Kant barely even made it out of Königsberg, they say that travel broadens the mind. Yet it's not the travel that does it. It's what you do with the travel. It's about how you use it to inform, affect and influence your thinking, if you'll let it.

So, as a result of my travels and experiences and my new life, I think about education and I think increasingly about injustice and I think about opportunity and the planet and I think about love and loss and life, and I think that just about covers most of what is important.

To sum up, then, this isn't so much a book about what I think but what you think. I hope you enjoy my thinking but please refrain from using it as a substitute for your own. Then it will all have been worthwhile.

42 Uses for This Book

1. To help you think.
2. To help you teach.
3. To help you think about teaching.
4. To help you teach about thinking.
5. As a graduation prize.
6. As a retirement prize.
7. As a raffle prize.
8. As a booby prize.
9. As a birthday present.
10. As a Christmas present.
11. In the staffroom.
12. In the waiting room.
13. In the living room.
14. In the little boy's room.
15. In the bath.
16. In the pub.
17. In bed.
18. In one go.
19. On the go.
20. On the train.
21. On the loo.
22. On a whim.
23. All the way through.
24. Dipping in and out.
25. Cover to cover.
26. Front to back.
27. Back to front.
28. Back to back.
29. To yourself.
30. To someone else.
31. To pass the time.
32. To make things happen.
33. To make things stop.
34. To stop a draught.

35. To stop the rot.

36. To stop a riot.

37. To start a riot.

38. To start a revolution.

39. To start a discussion.

40. To start a lesson.

41. To end a lesson.

42. As a lesson to us all.

Thunks[1]

Is being strong the same as refusing to be weak?

Does a newborn baby achieve anything?

Is a mum who is abusive towards you better than no mum?

Does a dog know if you've hurt it by accident?

Is an inside-out hat the same hat?

Is never longer than forever?

---

1 Thunk: *n*. 1. a beguiling question about everyday things that stops you in your tracks and helps you start to look at the world in a whole new light.

Real-Time History

In April 2013, the Boston Marathon was hit by a double bomb attack carried out by two Chechen brothers. Three days later, after killing a police officer in Massachusetts, they were tracked down by police and a shoot-out ensued in which one of the brothers was killed. Several hours later, after an intensive search, the surviving brother was found, seriously wounded and hiding in a boat in a residential district. Between the Monday of the marathon atrocity and the Thursday of the killing and capture of the brothers, there was also a fire and an explosion at a fertiliser processing plant in Texas which left 15 people dead, many injured and destroyed property in the vicinity.

There are two striking facts about how I know about these dramatic and tragic events.

The first is that I didn't read about it in the news. I don't read newspapers (if I want an opinion I'll come up with one and so I don't need to be fed one). I didn't watch them on some 24-hour rolling news channel. I don't have a TV. I didn't even read about it on a news website, although I could have done, eventually. I learned about the events the way I receive most of my news these days – through Twitter. And not tweets from the BBC or NBC or any formal news channel. Most of the above was through tweets and retweets put out by @YourAnonNews, the 'news' aggregation 'service' of the 'protest' 'group'

Anonymous[1] – the ones with the Guy Fawkes masks inspired by the film *V for Vendetta*.

The second is that I didn't so much read or hear about the terrible events in the US that week as actually witness them. When the fugitive brothers shot the policeman at Massachusetts Institute of Technology, I was one of the first to know, within minutes of it happening. When the entire city of Boston was on lockdown as heavily armed police officers and SWAT teams combed the streets, I was learning about it as it took place and 'watching' the drama as I 'peered out' from behind someone's net curtains. As it was happening. When the first gunfight took place, I watched through a narrow gap and heard the shots ringing out and the shouts of the police officers in the darkness. I watched the flames from the burning fertiliser plant near Waco from the front of an SUV, saw the massive explosion that followed and heard the screams of the child behind me as he cried to his dad, 'I can't hear! I can't hear! Get out of here! Please get out of here!' All within minutes of it happening.

I wasn't reading about these events in the news, I was experiencing history in real time.

9

---

1 Note how many quote marks I need to try to define, in old terms, a modern phenomenon that distributes news but is not a news service, that does protest but is not just about protests, and is a group in that there is more than one person behind it but it is not an organisation in the way that you or I would previously understand it.

There is a sense in which school-based history lessons are, at best, a process of understanding and interpreting historic events and their protagonists or, at worst, the memorisation and regurgitation of 'one f****** thing after another'. All well and good, but what about tomorrow's history? To what extent are you using the opportunities afforded through the instantaneous transmission of events by ordinary people experiencing those events to help your learners witness them for themselves and while the events are happening? To what extent are you mediating between your learners and the world as it unfolds, helping them grasp it, understand it, anticipate it, be affected by it, learn from it, act upon it even, and all in real time?

Observations

It's about love, life and death – all else is admin.

In a world where so few think, what counts is
not what you think but that you think.

I firmly believe you should do routine things in a different order each day so
that you don't notice the slow approach of death.

Some teachers define themselves by the number of rules they enforce;
some children by the number they break.

The Pigness of a Cow

'Look at that pig', I remember my 3-year-old daughter exclaiming, pointing excitedly across the ploughed field at the animal on the old railway embankment.

We were on one of those exercise-the-dog, bond-with-at-least-one-of-my-children, grab half-an-hour-with-nature walks that my youngest daughter would humour me by coming on. We both knew she would rather be at the park, the dog tied to the see-saw, so perhaps it was only the dog that was truly happy now.

The field was speckled green with the first fringe of next year's corn. The notion that, 'If we come back in a few months' time this will be as tall as you are' is a difficult concept for a 3-year-old, but then children are always far happier being with the here-and-now than the one-day-soon.

And what was here-and-now was that pig grazing quietly on the other side of the field. Except, of course, that it was a cow.

It was only as I was about to point out my daughter's mistake that I actually looked at the animal and realised why she had seen it as a pig. Or, to put it another way, noticed the pigness of the cow. It was clearly not a pig but I knew that not because of what it looked like – it did in fact have many pig-like features including pale skin and a stocky body on four skinny legs – but simply because

I knew that it was a cow. But sometimes it takes a 3-year-old to teach us to stop and see things how they really are and not just how we know them to be.

If you're a bird watcher, you know the excitement to be had in seeing a movement in a tree or bush, the millennia-old hunting instinct kicking in as you focus all your senses on that movement. As soon as the bird makes itself apparent as a chaffinch or a great tit, or whatever it happens to be, it is as if a large part of your brain switches off. You've named it now. End of. In many ways, the more I know the names of birds the less I know of birds.

When education becomes a spotting and labelling exercise we lose our ability to observe the world as it is. It is one of the mistakes I made with my Around Deeply project a few years ago where we sailed around the British Isles. The plan was to go and observe the world, as if seeing it for the first time, to see what everyone else had seen but to look deeply, as if with new eyes. Yet, by mistakenly engaging with well-meaning scientists it became a spotting and labelling exercise. I should have gone with my first idea and just taken artists. Artists and 3-year-olds. Then we would have really known what it was like to observe the world we live in. And at a far deeper level. Who knows, we may have even spotted the pigness of a dolphin.

Observations

A developing country can only develop as quickly as its slowest bureaucrats.

'This is a further final call for passengers …'
A glimpse of infinity in Dubai airport.

My advice to new teachers: stay out of the staffroom at lunchtime.

To say 'I don't deserve this' is to fall for the allure of the 'D' word.
It will only end in bitterness and frustration.

A Ten-Step Parent Guide to Supporting a Child's Learning in the Early Years

I was approached by a parent of a young child who asked for my advice when it came to supporting their child's learning. This is what I sent back. Like Justin Bieber, it's not the finished product but it's a start.

1. Self-esteem is the number one thing you can do for your child. A child who knows they can even if they don't yet know how has a chance. The child who thinks they can't because they don't yet know how will always be in trouble.

2. The best learning is multi-sensory and the younger the child, the more multi-sensory they are naturally ('Don't put that in your mouth!' 'Why not?' 'Because hamsters don't like it!'), so when it comes to learning, make sure they touch it, smell it, see it, taste it, hear it.

3. Young children and scientists have more than poor social skills in common. They have a passion for the 'why?' word. Encourage this.

4. Building on that, scientists work by formulating hypotheses about the way things are before trying to prove themselves right. This is a 'thinking to knowing' process. Encourage the same for children. Encourage them to put forward their own possible reasons as to why things are like they are and then to think about how they could be tested.

5. Linked to 'thinking to knowing' is Socratic dialogue. Socrates got his students to think by constantly challenging their assertions with questions. Do the same with children in a way that is encouraging and fun (yet that never undermines their self-confidence – remember self-esteem is key). This also encourages those all-important attributes resilience and concentration, sticking with an idea and not just giving up 'coz it's hard'.

6. The best learners are the ones who are interested in the world and one of the best ways to encourage this is to model it. Be interested yourself in everything around you and let your child see that.

7. Look for natural, everyday opportunities to do basic literacy and numeracy work – street signs, advertising hoardings, shops, TV. There are opportunities everywhere. Encourage word games, tongue-twisters, puns, rhymes, number puzzles, counting games, anything that helps children learn that words and numbers are endlessly interesting.

8. Keep it light. Make it fun. Celebrate achievement (celebrating with a high-five ritual is much better than bribing them with sweets).

9. School homework can be the death of family learning so handle with extreme caution. If you think it's rubbish and doing more harm than good then tell the teacher, but also tell them what you are going to do instead. You won't be very popular but then the school should be trying harder.

10. Did we mention self-esteem?

What's the Point of Education?

With anything in life, when you ask 'What's the point?', it remains a perfectly valid question even though there may be no answer. After all, having no answer doesn't mean the question is without merit. Far from it.

The process of asking questions is the release of a build-up. A cognitive eruption. One born from frustration, from dissatisfaction. From being hindered, blocked. From the universe being kinked somehow so you can no longer carry on along your way.

The process of asking questions means you've noticed. You're clever enough to have noticed. Clever enough to have framed a response that starts with 'Why is this like that?' That you have noticed a 'this' and a 'that' and an interaction between them, even if that interaction is a mismatch. So, feel good. You may receive an answer. You may receive an answer in the way distant future. You may never receive any response whatsoever. That's not the point. Questions are questions. Answers are different things altogether. Don't confuse them. Salt and pepper share a tabletop but they are not opposing sides of the same coin in the way that love and hate are.

'What's the point?' is a fair question. When it comes to your life, the answer is easy really. It is whatever you happen upon once you've asked the question. Asking a question, in turn, asks your brain to notice things. Like looking at the stars and seeing patterns. There are, of course, no patterns in the stars. But every star is part of whatever pattern you create at that moment. 'Look, there's a bull, a bear, a saucepan, the head gasket for a Triumph Herald.' That's the thing with stars. They can be whatever you want them to be. Like your life.

What's the point of education? Another good question. And, again, the answer is everything and nothing. And no one knows and everyone knows. The trouble is, so few people ask the question. And the more significant you are in determining the nature of how education is then, it seems, the less you bother asking the question about what it's for.

The thing with education and hairdressing, and unlike spot welding and accountancy, is that we've all been there. And for quite a while. Hours of our lives sitting still engaged in small talk to while away the boredom while the expert plies his or her craft. And hairdressing's not much better either. What this means is that everyone's an expert when it comes to education. There is little need for actual politicians to ask actual teachers anything about their work, their art, the actual craft of teaching. They know what good teaching is. It's what was going on when they were learning at school. And if they weren't learning, or if they didn't receive it, then it's not good teaching. It is an entirely logical standpoint. Like the doctor prescribing you medicine that works for her. And, obviously, not prescribing you those antibiotics to which she is allergic.

The sentence 'What works for me will work for you' contains one clause too many. The sentence 'What works for me is the right thing for everyone to have' is just a non sequitur. But it is an alluring one. Especially in education when there is no consensus to oppose it. Apart from narrow-minded ignorance (if that's not an oxymoron itself) such a position also assumes a conceited view of the speaker. And it is a view that lies invisibly between the two clauses. Start to ask questions about the logic in the statement and the conceit starts to appear. 'What works for me ...' brings with it an implication which is, 'Look at me. I'm great, me. More people like me, that's what's needed. Now, in order to achieve that you need to have gone through what I went through, in particular, my school days, which played such a great part in my formation. So let's put you through that too because, after all, it works so it will work for you.'

20   Education therefore becomes the process by which we generate people like us. Which is precisely the last thing it should be.

People like us are the ones who have made the mess, created the tensions, perpetuated the old arguments, pooped in our own fanny packs. Why on earth do we need more people like us? What the earth needs is people who are not like us. Not at all. It doesn't need people like us and it doesn't need them now.

Which allows us to reposition our view about the point of education. What it isn't about is producing more people like us, people who share our knowledge, our values, our codes. People who, in short, think like us. That way, like the population of Easter Island trying to outdo each other in being more Rapa Nui than the rest of the Rapa Nui, we're all doomed.

Which means the purpose of education is to help create people who can think for themselves. Which means we don't care how they look. How they behave. How they learn. How they dream. How they think. We just want to ensure that they do think. Deeply. And for themselves.

Now, this is something very different from rearing monsters. Not enforcing our code upon them doesn't mean they leave school without codes. Far from it. Not subjecting to them our view of morality doesn't mean we are producing amoral young people. We are not encouraging not thinking. We are encouraging them to think for themselves, something that entails some serious reflection on what is right and wrong, what is good and proper, what is the appropriate thing to do and for whom.

For example, a discussion that has 'Is it right to bully a bully?' as its starting point not only helps young people develop thinking skills and other competencies – such as the ability to debate, to persuade, to listen, to have a point of view, to articulate it, to put it out there for scrutiny, to stand by it but, if necessary, to reject it – it also helps young people develop a moral code for themselves. This is very different from having one foisted upon them. Who are we to press a moral code upon anyone anyway? They are such fickle things. Jean Valjean stole a loaf of bread and ended up in prison. He broke the law. Serves him right. He knew the rules. James Lulham of Sussex was hanged for stealing a sheep. Serves him right. He knew the code. He was lucky though. His brother committed the same offence and was sent to Australia.

But surely 'Thou shalt not kill' is an absolute? We can teach that code at least? In Chile, dictator Augusto Pinochet oversaw the death of more than 3,000 people. There are plenty of Chilean citizens – people who go to church, who love their children, who give money to charity – who are fully able to justify those actions. After all, they were 'for the greater good' of the country, not to mention their own status and pockets. 'Thou shalt not abduct, torture, rape, disappear, murder, bury in mass graves by the sea. Except …' The mayor of one affluent part of Santiago held a ceremony on his patch in 2011 to celebrate the life and achievements of Brigadier General Miguel Krassnoff, one of Pinochet's henchmen. The Brigadier General wasn't able to attend though, what with him serving 144 years for murder and kidnap.

Given the opportunity to discuss, to reflect, to empathise, to think, children do. And they come up with better conclusions than we do. Teaching them to think is very different from simply teaching them to be clever. The economic crisis that most of the world is enduring is not the result of a deficit in intellect. Nor is the environmental one. Some very clearly, very clever people are at work in both of these instances.

Which is why the teaching of thinking – that is, how to think and not what to think, as Dewey contested 100 years ago – is up there in a modern trivium. To read and write; to do numbers; to think. Everything else they can sort for themselves these days (and yes, I am referring to technology).

A call for teaching children to think in schools isn't, please let's be clear about this, a call for having thinking lessons in schools. As soon as you put a subject into a box like that it becomes notoriously difficult to achieve 'transfer', to move the discipline outside the box it came in and into other boxes that litter the school day. So, don't fence it in. All teachers are teachers of thinking if they only let themselves. The more we can help teachers help children think for themselves the better. And one of the key ways we can do this is to stop thinking for them. 'Don't ride the bike for them' as a teacher once told me. Don't finish their sentences when they're struggling to formulate an idea. Don't rush them on when they need time to think (remember the 'wait time' rule – three seconds is all you need to give). Don't underestimate their abilities. Don't confuse memory with intelligence. Don't confuse speaking and participating. Don't assume if they're not speaking out they're not thinking hard. (Often those who speak most think least.) Don't think you need to talk more to get them to think more. 'Come on, think!' is an exhortation as useful as 'Come on, speak Polish!' or 'Come on, be thin!'

Pepper your teaching with 'In your opinion …', 'What do you think?', ' What does that mean to you?', 'What would you do if you were …?', 'What would happen if …?', 'Why do you say that?', 'Do you agree?', 'What does that mean?', 'I don't know', 'What would that lead to?', 'Where did that thought come from?', 'Guess!', 'What could that mean?', 'What may happen next?' 'What could an answer be?', 'How would you solve the problem?', 'What do you think it means?', 'What do you feel is right?', 'Who do you feel is right?', 'Do you disagree?', 'Why do you think that?', 'Why did they think that?', 'How sure are you that is the right answer?', 'What is your solution to …?', 'How might others see this?', 'Is that your best answer or your first answer?', 'How does this link with …?', 'When might that not be true?', 'Where might that not be true?', 'Have another guess?', 'What if the opposite were true?', 'Could the opposite be true?', not to mention the powerful 'I disagree with you, persuade me'.

In our more erudite halls of learning, such questioning has been taking place for centuries. But hoi polloi are to be kept that way in order to ensure that they don't ask such questions. Paulo Freire, in *Pedagogy of the Oppressed*, cites a Mr Davies Giddy, president of the UK's Royal Society, on educating such lower members of society:

> *For, however specious in theory the project might be, of giving education to the labouring classes of the poor, it would, in effect, be found to be prejudicial to their morals and happiness; it would teach them to despise their lot in life instead of making them good servants in agriculture, and other laborious employments to which their rank in society had destined them; instead of teaching them subordination, it would render them fractious and refractory, as was evident in the manufacturing counties; it would enable them to read seditious pamphlets, vicious books, and publications against Christianity; it would render them insolent to their superiors and, in a few years, the result would be, that the legislature would find it necessary to direct the strong arm of power towards them.*[1]

But that was then. Education may have had a different point and purpose then. We are playing to different rules now. Or at least some of us are trying to.

---

1   Hansard, HC Deb. (series 1), vol. 9, col. 798 (13 June 1807). Quoted in P. Freire, *Pedagogy of the Oppressed* (New York: Continuum, 1970).

Thunks

Is it more important to do 'I love you' than to say 'I love you'?

If I read the English translation and you read the Spanish translation are we both reading the same book?

Can the worst thing that has ever happened to you also be the best?

With every new song written does that mean there will be fewer new songs left to write?

In China, workers live, work and sleep in the factory used by Apple, so could you say iPhones are 'home made'?

If you built a railway line that did converge on the horizon could you tell?

Advice I

Iwas recently asked to give an address to a group of graduating International Baccalaureate students at a prestigious international school near London. This is what I wished I had been told and what I share with my children (when they listen).

Laugh. Life, like education, is too important to be taken seriously.

Love yourself. Mind and body. If you don't love yourself, why should anyone else? It's dangerous enough out there without you being a danger to yourself.

Hug with both hands. Your family will not be around forever. Embrace them as you embrace life. Fully.

Serve. However little you have, it will be more than most. Ensure your life makes other people's lives better. Somehow.

You can until you can't. And then you still can. Don't let anyone put artificial limits on what you are capable of achieving. Including yourself. Often what seems like a wall is just a door. And even if it is a wall, treat it like a door anyway.

Be someone. Don't be anyone. Ensure the universe knows you have existed.

Observations

Every day, when you see your gods, you must remember to say thank you. They are like parents in that way. You receive far more from them when you don't ask them for anything but instead thank them for all they have given you already.

When teachers talk about education they are referring to what they can get out of young people. When politicians talk about it they are referring to what they can put into young people. It's important to remember this difference.

There are times when you have to look around
at all your possessions and say, 'It's just stuff'.

Facts are what we construct our truths with. So, let's teach children
to be careful about where they find their facts.

On Feedback

The very first time I was exposed to any form of critical feedback in a professional way was when I was working in advertising. One of our ideas (to promote the wide range of Formica work surface colours with the tagline 'Obstacle course for chameleons') had been sent off to a panel to be assessed. What came back said more about the likes and dislikes of the panel of reviewers than it did about our ideas.

It was from this point that I realised that any form of critical feedback is not so much a magnifying glass held up to your work but a mirror reflecting the reviewer's own preferences, prejudices and limitations.

I don't use, advocate or look at the 'happy sheets' that schools and organisations tend to use at the end of a day's training. If 99 out of 100 come back as positive, human nature dictates that it is the single bad one that makes the journey home a process of self-flagellation. If the feedback is more evenly spread, what does that say about anything? If 50 people liked what you did and 50 people didn't, there is nothing to be learned from that except the preferences of each group. And if everyone thought the day was dire, you should have known that far earlier and either done something about it or one or both parties should have walked away at lunchtime while they had the chance.

If I were to put out a 'happy sheet' it would have two numbers on it – 1 and 10. Nothing in between. 'It was rubbish!' is a far more gratifying piece of feedback than 'It was OK'.

An Alternative
Good School Checklist

Call me fussy, but one of the schools that I would least want my children to go to is one of the most expensive, prestigious and academically high-achieving schools I've ever seen.

But then I have high expectations when it comes to a decent education for my children.

When parents, MPs, estate agents or the media refer to a 'good school', it is usually on the basis of exam results, league table positions (which are based on exam results) or inspection reports (which take into account exam results).[1]

Yet, there is so much more to what makes a good school and we need to keep our eye on these other aspects for fear of losing them in the 'race to the top'. To help, I would like to suggest a 25-point 'good school' checklist to help us all focus on a bigger picture.

1. Do children enjoy going there?
2. Do teachers enjoy going there?

---

1 Or price. After all, with education there is an assumption that if you are paying for it then it is better than schooling that is free, which we know is not always the case.

3. Are all children challenged by the work?

4. Do the children develop competencies as well as earn grades?

5. Do the children learn skills as well as facts?

6. Are morals and values focused on and exhibited daily by all members of the school community?

7. Is there an inclusive atmosphere where all children are valued for who they are and what they bring?

8. Are key issues like bullying and other social and emotional aspects of school life discussed and addressed in a positive, open way?

9. Is the ability to think for themselves encouraged and developed in all children?

10. Does the school have a sense of fun?

11. Are aspects like wonder, curiosity, adventure, bravery, resilience and resistance actively encouraged and celebrated?

12. Are the teachers open to new ideas and keen to do things with – and not to – the learners?

13. Does the school keep up to date with new advances in learning?

14. Does the school keep up to date with new advances in learning technology?

15. Are high expectations of the children matched by high expectations of the staff?

16. Is the head teacher visible?

17. Are children taught that being their best doesn't have to involve being better than others?

18. Is the unexpected welcomed?

19. Do children get to think about, interact with and seek to change life outside of the school walls?

20. Is the school aware that learning is something that children can do at anytime, anywhere and only part of it needs to be within the school walls?

21. Does the school community extend beyond the school?

22. Do the lessons incorporate a variety of learning opportunities and possibilities?

23. Do the children have the opportunity to be responsible for something and take decisions that make a difference?

24. Are the results sufficient enough to allow all children to go to the next stage of their life, whatever that may be?

25. Does the lady[2] on reception smile at visitors?

---

2   In my considerable experience of visiting schools it is usually a lady. Don't shoot the messenger.

Observations

A developed country boasts great schools.
A developing country boasts great shopping centres.

Technology not working properly for young people is like gravity
stopping for the older generation.

You can't look out of both windows of the train at the same time.

Love me, love my love.

Indignez-vous – Et Eux

Want to know one of my biggest regrets? It's not getting beaten up in a college bar in Durham University when I was 20.

It was just before closing time and, in the queue for the late-night toastie bar, a rugby-playing oaf of a toff was drunkenly picking on a guy half his size whom I suspected of being involved in some form of higher maths. There is something about the moneyed classes, not just in the UK but around the world, that seems to endow them with a sense of self-superiority they do not merit. Some of the most physically ugly people I have ever seen were so rich they didn't even know it. I don't know but I suspect the bully, these days, is high up in some private investment bank. The little guy is probably involved in some form of higher maths.

The thing is, I, and everyone else in the crowded bar, just watched as the drunken bully picked on and pushed around the unfortunate undergraduate who had simply come in for a toasted cheese-and-pickle sandwich before bed. I remember it vividly and I remember vividly what I did too. Nothing. I saw injustice. I saw violence. I saw a wrong being committed. And I did nothing.

Who knows what would have happened had I stepped into the fray. Earlier that night, I had seen the bully down a pint of beer in a matter of seconds and smash the empty glass against his own empty head, gashing his forehead in the process. Somehow I don't think a reasoned debate would have followed if I had stood up to him with an indignant, 'Now then, fine fellow, enough of that …' What I now know is that whatever may have happened as a consequence of my actions, if I had taken any, is irrelevant. It is the fact that I did something that would have counted. Even if he had beaten us both within an inch of our lives with a smouldering sandwich toaster, it wouldn't have mattered now. Those wounds would heal. It is the shame I feel for having done nothing that will never go away. The scars of the fight I never had are the ones I can't get rid of.

It is not my intention to let that happen again.

The French Resistance fighter Stéphane Hessel wrote a book that inspired a whole generation around the world to get cross and fight back.[1] *Indignez-vous!* is a rallying cry to young people everywhere to find injustice – 'Look around you, you will find there the issues that justify your indignation' – and then to do something to change it. Doing nothing is the worst possible path to take – after all, 'the worst of all attitudes is indifference'.

What message are we sharing with young people? Is 'turn the other cheek' another way of saying 'look the other way'? Would you condone a young person being involved in civil unrest if that person reasonably felt that this was the

---

1 S. Hessel, *Indignez-vous!* (Montpellier: Editions Indigène, 2011).

only course of action open to them in order to make a point to a government (or school leadership) that it was not doing the job it was supposed to? Do you agree with Hessel's point that, although not condoning terrorism, as does Sartre, he does understand it as 'a form of exasperation'? Is taking action to try and put right a perceived wrong a punishable offence in your household or school? Is life easier if you simply sit in the bar and watch the big guy beat up the little guy? What if doing nothing is that for which you punish your children most?

Observations

You shouldn't be scared of death. After all, what's the worst that can happen?

The size of the hole is determined by the size of what
isn't the hole. Or is it the other way round?

If the tail is going to wag the dog, at least design a word-class tail.

You will do anything to make your children happy when you can't
prevent them from being sad.

How to Write a Book

I

The first step is to work out of it's a book in the first place. If you're not sure then follow these simple guidelines:

If you've got something to say write a tweet.
If you've got something to share write a blog.
If you've got something to change write a book.

II

Write the book that no one else could have written.

III

Never write the same book twice.

IV

The time the reader spends reading your book is a gift, given by the reader to you. It needs to be reciprocated. If the reader receives nothing from you, then you are no more than a thief.

Does It Know?

Does it know what it does
A rhinoceros?
Does it care for its grey hide
And horn?

Does a laughing hyena
Know that it's been a
Hyena from when
It was born?

Does a purposeful porpoise
Feel smugger than others?
Does a jellyfish wish
To breathe air?

Does the owl give two hoots
Of its station in life?
Does a leopard with spots
Really care?

Do ocelots floss a lot
To make an impression?
Does the otter care a jot
Of the time?

Is a llama with karma
More of a charmer?
Does a rat know of
Reason or rhyme?

Is an ambitious but vicious
Dog highly suspicious
Of the wants that it
Cannot afford?

Do the pole cats that goal set
Eat more mice than most?
Does the hummingbird hum
Coz it's bored?

Is the mind of a panda
A ceaseless meander
As it sits slowly chewing bamboo?

Does a skate contemplate
What it has on its plate?
Can a gnat get the gall
Of a gnu?

And then

The swan in the field
Under thundering skies
A cloud of intensity white
Beak beading with water
Wings full 'gainst the grey
Does it really sit dreaming of light?

Does it know that it is?
What it does, where it's been?
Does it think of what isn't, not now?

It is what it is, none the more,
none the less,
But does it know that it isn't a cow?

Observations

Always watch out for people who promise to be 'succinct'
when they could have said 'brief'.

If you have to wear your values on a lanyard, they're probably not your values.

I hope I will remain poor enough to grow old gracefully.

'I hope it works out for you' is what people say when they know you have a
problem in your life but, really, they don't give a toss.

You Don't Want Quits

In business, if you deliver what you get paid to deliver then the moral transaction between you and your client has been fulfilled. You promised to deliver. They promised to pay. You delivered what you promised. They paid as promised. Call it quits.

You don't want quits. Quits is bad for business.

If, on the other hand, you deliver more than they were expecting, more than they paid for, then they owe you. Not financially but morally. And if they owe you, they will come back to you, because most people are decent people.

It's the same if, for example, a prospective client makes a very last-minute cancellation. They will normally ask if there is a cancellation fee and offer to pay at least something for your time up to this point. It would be quite reasonable to charge them such a fee. After all, you have incurred costs. Not to mention the 'opportunity cost', that is to say, the time spent on what turned out to be a fruitless project when you could have been involved with a profitable one. As soon as you do accept their money, however, you are quits again. But you don't want quits, remember. Instead, you simply decline their offer of payment. That way they owe you. And, as most people are decent people, and those who aren't you wouldn't want to work with anyway, they will be back, if not tomorrow then next year or even many years down the line.

If you make any decision purely about chasing the money then, before long, every decision becomes about chasing the money. And that is a slippery slope – one that guarantees you will miss out on many opportunities. When you make every business transaction a moral one, not a purely financial one, then there are only two rules that apply: (a) stick to the moral high ground at all times, even if it loses you money and (b) don't settle for quits.

Observations

If every shop is exclusive then none of them are.

New social media provides the means by which people with something to say can say it, but not the wherewithal.

If a government is underperforming you can vote it out at the next general election, but what are you supposed to do if the Opposition is floundering? Perhaps the greatest rebuke would be to vote them in.

Integrity is knowing which principles to compromise first.

It Will Only Take One Word
to End Cake Sales for Good

If you must have a cake sale to raise money for some deserving charity then may I suggest a slightly different angle? Apart from spending time ensuring the children involved understand what their money is going to and how it is going to be used, you could also encourage them to ask why the situation is so bad that their baking skills are being called on in the first place.

For example, if you are 'raising money for Africa', as seems to be so often the case, why is it that a continent with such a wealth of natural resources is home to so many of the world's poor? How is it that some of the very communities you are trying to help are not only sitting on vast reserves of oil, gas, diamonds and gold (not to mention various substances that go into making the mobile phone in your pocket), but that the individual children and families you are trying to support are actually involved in mining these minerals? Why are there repeated famines in certain countries? Why are people starving in countries where there is enough food to go round? If so many of these countries are so poor and wretched, why did the European empires go to war to have their 'place in the sun' and possess these same countries not that long ago? Does having these countries poor have its benefits for the rich countries? What would happen if these countries became as 'developed' as say the UK or the US?

If you are raising money to help the poor in India, Pakistan, Bangladesh or across the Indian subcontinent, what was the role of the British Empire in these countries? Where did these countries come from and how? Did they become British colonies so we could help them out? What did Britain gain from them? Or indeed take from them? How was it that we colonised them and not the other way around? Did the region need charity before the British arrived? If so, where did it come from? If not, why not?

Or what if you are raising money to help the poor of South America? Again, why are there so many poor in a continent with so many natural resources under their feet? Why are the poor people in that part of the world always dark skinned yet the people who run the businesses and the countries lighter skinned? Is any of the wealth we enjoy as a country due, even if only in part, to the fact that there are so many people who remain poor in that part of the world?

What if you are baking cakes to save endangered animals? Why are they endangered? Who or what is endangering them? Is anything we are doing in our day-to-day lives the very thing that is causing these animals to be endangered? If fish stocks are low due to over-fishing, who is over-fishing, who is over-profiting, who is losing out and what will the fishermen do if they can't fish? If elephants and rhinos are in danger due to poaching, who is doing the poaching and why? What would those people do if they didn't earn money from poaching? Where does the money come from to pay them for their poaching?

If you are raising money due to some great 'natural disaster' then how much of a natural disaster is it, really? Is that famine or flood an 'Act of God' or the result of global warming? How come that earthquake left the rich end of town virtually untouched yet devastated the poor end of town? Was Haiti just unfortunate to have had such a bad earthquake in 2010 or were there events that took place years, decades or centuries ago that made the impact of the earthquake so much more severe? Were the predominantly poor and black people of New Orleans who were most affected by Hurricane Katrina just unfortunate to be in the wrong place at the wrong time?

Every disaster, every case of extreme need, every instance of severe human suffering, is the result of some chain of events. While doing what is necessary to help is, of course, a good thing, as is encouraging a sense of collective responsibility and compassionate citizenship in young people, failing to look beyond the event is neglectful when it comes to educating our young people properly. By matching each act of charity with an attempt to understand how things got to be so bad, we may even begin to break the cycle in years to come. In this way, asking 'why?' could be the greatest act of charity we can perform.

Trust Your Gut

The best way to know if the idea you have just had is a good one or not is to be aware of what your immediate gut reaction is. There is a neurological delay between what you think and actually thinking about what you think, but it is a delay that your belly doesn't experience. So learn to trust it. After all, when you look back, there are many stupid ideas that your brain has talked you into when left to its own devices.

Don't Let Them Tell You

Don't let them tell you that the only way of measuring what you do is to test what they know. Testing is the approach to education that those who know the least about education prefer most. You can put results into a spreadsheet and wave it in the faces of voters. Harder to do the same with the personal growth of individual children. If your goal is to turn schools into factories where children without qualifications go in and young people with qualifications come out, then you will want processes that can be measured. But there are other successful models, ones not built on Taylorism. Finland, for example, where there are no national tests until the end of high school. But then Finnish education isn't yet being groomed to be handed over to Big Business. And testing for facts is cheap. Not only that, it is big business.

If you know that education is more than the sum of its measurable outcomes, just follow the mantra, 'Cover your back and sleep at night'. Do what you need to do to get through the hoops, but do more than get through hoops.

Don't let them tell you that teaching is a straightforward 'cause and effect' process whereby children learn what you teach them. Again, if you want a factory model that needs measurable outcomes to operate, then testing the extent to which young people have in their heads the 'canon' that was in your head is fine. But education is much more than that. And far more complex.

Understanding the glorious complexity involved in the education process needs intelligent, thinking, reflective professionals. They are expensive though. Expensive to train. Expensive to maintain. Especially when, again, the system is being dumbed down to be sufficiently cheap to run in such a way that Big Business can make a profit. Far better to have the educational equivalent of lever pullers. There are plenty of them waiting to come into the job.

What can you do? For a start, think about what you do and how you do it. Treat every lesson as an experiment. Do things with children and not to them. Talk, read, share, blog, tweet. Stand up as a professional educator.

Secondly, don't let them tell you that your subject isn't as valuable as someone else's. For one, English and maths aren't important for everyone, but literacy and numeracy are. And you can make plenty of room for them, whatever your discipline.

Thirdly, think about the core skills you want your children to develop – team working, leadership, problem spotting and solving, resilience, persuasion, fine motor skills and the like. Build specific opportunities for these into your planning. They transcend any prejudice about your subject area.

And fourth, children's brains are not compartmentalised. Doing well in your subject has spin-offs for them everywhere. People with a second language have been shown to be more creative. Developing fine motor skills is important for neurological development, as is learning to play a musical instrument. Confidence in sport or drama reappears elsewhere. The powers that be might not think your subject counts. That just gives you the freedom to show that it does.

If you stand by and let them tell you any of these things, they will not only continue to tell you but they will even start to think they are right. They aren't. Don't let them tell you they are.

Thunks

Can a state love its people and, if so, should it?

If there are more humans in the world now than ever before, are there fewer molecules around to be used to make other things?

Is there a safe way to die?

Can you please someone without making them happy?

If the wrapper is in my pocket is it litter?

If you are locked out of your car is it broken down?

Can you be as sure something you can't see doesn't exist as you can be that it does?

Independent Thinking
as a Refusal

When it comes to being creative, stand by my motto: do things no one does or do things everyone does but in a way no one does. Follow this advice and you arrive at the heart of independent thinking, at the understanding that the first step to being creative is not an act of creation, or even destruction, as Picasso would have it, but one of refusal.

To refuse to do it like others have done it.

To refuse to think the obvious thought.

To refuse to countenance the response that others would accept.

To refuse to tread in footsteps.

To refuse to blend in.

To refuse to use – or indeed be – a cliché.

To refuse to compromise.

To refuse to do the obvious.

To refuse to be weak.

To refuse to write on lined paper.

To refuse to take the coach to the party.[1]

To refuse routine.

To refuse to work hard.

To refuse the easy option.

To refuse to subside.

To refuse the mainstream media.

To refuse high street shops.

To refuse designer labels.

To refuse to be 'JohnSmith475' on Twitter or Gmail.

To refuse to watch Sir Ken Robinson's TED Talks – or anyone else's for that matter.

To refuse to drive a Vauxhall.

To refuse package deals.

To refuse to wear slippers.

And to refuse the unremitting pressure to accept all of the above.

I didn't say it was easy.

---

1   'Gregariousness is always the refuge of mediocrities', says Nikolai Nikolaevich Vedeniapin in Boris Pasternak's *Doctor Zhivago*, quoted in Freire, *Pedagogy of the Oppressed*, who saw it rather as 'an imprisoning armor which prevents men from loving'.

Observations

Creativity starts with 'If only ...' Mediocrity ends with it.

Inspire from the front, lead from the middle, observe from the
rear and undermine from the sides.

Don't ask your god for health or wealth or happiness. Those things lie either
in your hands or in the hands of fate or both. Instead ask for the one thing
that you can be assured of receiving simply by asking – strength.

There are no domains in independent thinking. Everything is linked.

Observations

Being average has its place, but it's not for everyone.

There are some events that are too important to be a
photograph and should remain a memory.

Identifying and changing what's ineffective is easier
than identifying and changing what's inefficient.

When confronted with any new opportunity the best approach is to ask
yourself, 'Will I regret not having attempted this?' Then whether to do it or
not becomes a simple question of yes or no.

On Starting a Revolution

A short story based on a true story

I

The little boy didn't mean to start a revolution. He had just said, politely but firmly, that no, he wouldn't write down anything during the test the teacher was giving the class one afternoon that autumn.

His teacher, Señora Ortiz, wasn't sure quite what to make of this stance. At first she thought he was joking and had simply smiled at him and responded by saying that was all very funny but would he now start writing down his answers on the paper in front of him like the rest of the class. She had then wandered off to look over the shoulders of the other children who all had their heads down and were writing away furiously or, in the case of the Hernández twins, not writing very much as usual and not appearing that bothered by the fact.

When she glanced back towards the boy a few minutes later and realised that he wasn't joking, she took a firmer line and, walking back to his desk, she raised herself to her full height in front of it, her lips thinning visibly, and told him that he simply must do what he was told and get on with the test. After an awkward pause while the boy struggled to work out if that was one instruction or two and the teacher struggled to maintain the height she had just attained, the little boy quietly mumbled that no, he didn't want to. And that was that.

'Are you telling me that you haven't prepared for this test, young man? Is that why you aren't writing anything?' the teacher began. 'You've known for weeks that it was coming up.' Her line of questioning and her tone of voice revealed a history of having trodden this path before, coupled with an ignorance of the fact that she was treading new ground this time.

'No, Señora. I was up late last night going over it and I even had my mother helping me.'

'So, you *do* know the answers then?'

'Yes, of course I do.'

'Then write them down then,' Señora Ortiz persisted, 'that way I will know that you know the answers.'

'Don't you believe me then, Señora? Don't you think I know the answers?'

'It's not a question of whether I *believe* you or not,' she replied, emphasising the word 'believe' as if she was trying to prove a point to someone who wasn't in the room.

'So you do believe me?' the boy replied.

'Well, yes, of course I do. I know you're a good little boy and you wouldn't lie to me.'

'So, it's OK then?'

'No! No, it's not OK, young man.'

'Why is it not OK?'

'Because knowing is one thing, knowing you know is another, and showing me you know is something else altogether.'

The boy hesitated whilst he thought through his teacher's logic, then with a confident smile he replied, 'That's easy enough then …'

'What do you mean?'

'Just ask me a question and I'll tell you.'

The teacher had started to become a little frustrated at the way this conversation was going or, to put it another way, with the fact that it wasn't going in the direction she had intended it to go. What's more, the other children were beginning to prick up their ears, curious to hear where this dialogue was going.

'No,' said the teacher, trying to hide her impatience in a way that made it clear she was impatient and trying to hide it. 'I … need you … to write … the answer … down.'

'Why?' persisted the boy, not out of malice but out of persistence.

'Because that way … I can take it away and read it later.'

'But if I just tell you now it will save you having to take it away and read it later, won't it?'

'Well, yes, it will, but that's not the point.'

'So, what is the point then, Señora?'

'The point is that I have asked you to revise for a test …'

'Yes …'

'Which means that I then give you that test …'

'Yes …'

'Which you then answer …'

'By writing the answers on this paper?'

'Yes, by writing down all you know on that bit of paper so I can see how well you have learned what I have been teaching you for the last few weeks.'

'Are you worried that you are not very good then, Señora?' asked the boy in all innocence.

'What do you mean?' replied Señora Ortiz shirtily.

'I mean, are you checking to see how well I have learned it because you are not very sure how well you have taught it?'

'Don't be so rude!' snapped Señora Ortiz, trying not to raise her voice and disturb the rest of the class but doing it in such a way that the rest of the class knew something was going on and were now starting to glance up from their test papers.

The little boy looked genuinely shocked that his teacher thought he was being rude and his face fell.

'I wasn't being rude, Señora Ortiz, I …'

'I know, I know …' said Señora Ortiz, trying to calm things down again quickly. 'I know. Now, if you …' She stopped and looked around, standing there in the middle of the classroom, all eyes on her. 'If we *all* can just get on with our tests …' All eyes returned to their papers. All eyes, that is, except for those of the little boy.

'Well …?' said the teacher, expecting to have won the battle. She indicated with a nod of her head that he should pick up his pen and make a start now without any more fuss. He was sitting with his back against his chair, his eyes fixed on his desk and, with a shrug, made it clear that nothing had changed and that he was not going to write down his answers.

'We are going to sort this out later, young man,' said the teacher crossly and left the boy to it. He sat and, staring out of the window at the last few leaves falling from the playground's one almost bare tree, quietly went through the answers to the questions in his head.

II

'So, are you saying that he refused to sit the test, Señora Ortiz?' asked the head teacher, on the verge of being cross, professionally speaking, but knowing that he needed to check the facts first. He had been wrong once before and he didn't want to go there again.

'That's right,' the teacher replied, looking at the little boy with just a hint of triumph in her voice, like someone who had just seen an unwanted cat chased off their garden by a dog, their dog. She had taken him by the hand to the head teacher's office as soon as the lesson had finished and she had collected in the other children's test papers. 'He simply refused to sit the test. I don't know what's come over him …'

'But Señora Ortiz,' the boy began to protest, 'I didn't refuse to sit the test.'

'So, you *did* the test?' asked the head teacher, starting to become unsure of himself again.

'Yes!' said the boy. 'No!' said his teacher at the same time.

The head teacher started to look cross now. He was the sort of man for whom it was important that others knew that he didn't have time to waste on things that weren't important to him.

'*Did* you sit the test, boy?' he asked, peering over the top of a desk full of half-read reports whilst Señora Ortiz stared at him with a thin mouth and hard eyes.

'I did the test, Señor …' the boy began, trying to let the truth speak for itself without his fear or confusion getting in the way. His eyes were on the stained carpet at his feet but he was aware of those of his teacher burning into his neck from where she sat across the office from him. 'I just didn't write the answers down, Señor.'

'What do you mean, you did the test but didn't write the answers down?' said the head teacher, both answering and asking the same question.

'I did the test, Señor, I just did it in my head.'

Señora Ortiz turned her look of triumph up another notch and sat there, her eyes on the head teacher, expectantly, her hands crossed on her lap.

III

The following day, the little boy found himself back in the head teacher's office with Señora Ortiz and the head teacher, again staring down at the stains on the carpet and the piece where the threads from underneath were starting to show through. This time he had his mother with him too. The line of questioning had not changed.

The head teacher was speaking in a way that proved he was in control to most of the people in the room. 'And are you prepared, young man, to tell your mother why you did not sit …, er, why you did not *write down*' (he emphasised these words as if he were pulling a splinter out of a child he didn't like) 'your answers to the test that Señora Ortiz had prepared for you?'

The little boy looked at his mother for reassurance and for strength. She did her best to deliver both, but there was also the need to look stern and reassure the other adults that this child of hers was still, if not under her direct control, at least subject to her influence.

'Well?' she said carefully.

'What's the point?' the boy began earnestly. 'I know the answers. You know I know the answers. Señora Ortiz says she believes me when I say I know the answers. What's the point of writing them down?'

'Because that way, dear,' began the little boy's mother, looking rather hesitantly at the head teacher and then at Señora Ortiz, 'your teacher can give you a mark to show you how well you have learned everything.'

'But she could do that by asking me the questions too.'

'I know, but there are other children in the class too and it would take a long time for them all to tell Señora Ortiz what they know.'

'And the way schools know how good they are at teaching things to children like you is to get them to write down all the things the teacher has taught them,' joined in Señora Ortiz.

'Not to mention the fact that the government compiles a big list of which schools have done well, so without you writing down your answers to Señora Ortiz's test we won't know if we're better than all the other schools,' added the head teacher.

The word the boy replied with was what really started the revolution, which caused the rest of the children to screw up their test papers and throw them out of the window, which led to the world's press coming to the school doors, which bankrupted exam boards, closed universities and brought down education ministers.

The boy looked at the head teacher and then at Señora Ortiz and then, finally, at his mother. Quietly he said , 'So …?'

Thunks

Can you wash a hole?

Is a stick dead?

If you turn a box upside down does the air inside go upside down too?

Should you live each life as if it were your last?

Is fighting for rights the same as fighting for justice?

Is equality the same as fairness?

Does a bad government encourage citizenship more than a good government?

Learning Makes Your Brain Fat

When I was writing my Google book[1] my brain became fat. The process of researching all the information that is in that book filled my head with so much 'stuff' that I found my delivery in training sessions became much slower and more stilted. There was so much I could say on a topic that I found I could actually say very little. Fortunately, nature has a great plan for circumstances such as this – it's called forgetting. By forgetting much of what I wrote I was able to get on with my life. If I hadn't then … Sentence. Stringing. Together. Hard. Would. Be. Still.

On the plus side, it means I can read my own book, should I feel the need, and learn new things each time.

---

1   I. Gilbert, *Why Do I Need a Teacher When I've Got Google?* (London: Routledge, 2012).

Drawing Class

The teacher was helping a class of 13-year-olds to write their own French poetry, which they were then asked to illustrate. It made a change from buying cabbages or asking the way to the ironmongers, neither of which the teacher had ever been called on to do in any country he had either visited or lived in. He was sitting at his desk and keeping out of their way so as not to let his teaching get in the way of their creativity when a girl came up to him with her pen and paper. She asked him to draw her a lump of clay as she wanted to use it for her poem. The teacher refused to do it, but instead asked her to close her eyes and visualise a table in her mind's eye. Once she had done this, he asked the girl to visualise a banana and a lump of clay on the table. Her eyes tightly shut, she nodded that she had done this.

'Great,' said the teacher, 'now draw the thing that isn't the banana.'

Observations

Life is a rollercoaster – you spend ages waiting for your turn, you spend most of the time either screaming or feeling sick and at the end of it your legs are shaky and you vow to never put yourself through such an ordeal ever again.

If you are a man of a certain age, there will be a hair growing out of your nostril and you would do well to remove it. If you fail to do so, any conversation between us will predominantly be one between me and it.

I had a bruise and prayed for it to heal and it did, thus proving there is a God. It took Him four weeks though.

Love is a verb.

Of Ducks and Lighthouses

'So, I said to this duck …' Such was the opening line to the very first INSET I ever delivered.

It was to the staff of the school in which I was working at the time and I had been asked to contribute to a whole-school training day on differentiation. Earlier that week, I had sat at my desk for about an hour penning a particularly erudite and worthy presentation, the sort of presentation that epitomised the word 'INSET'. Worthy, dull, dry, theoretical and humourless. An overhead projector was to be used throughout.

But then anyone can do that. Anyone with the courage to speak in public and the bottle to stand before a group of fellow professionals who all know they could do better. Independent thinking, though, starts with a refusal, if you remember. That and the constant belief that there must be another way.

Which is when the line that had suddenly and randomly come into my head came into play. 'So, I said to this duck …'

And that was enough. The remainder of the presentation ran easily from my pen and, if I remember rightly, involved a whole host of school characters being interviewed by a duck to get to the bottom of differentiation in the classroom.

I mention this story for two reasons and not simply to highlight yet another use for a duck. Firstly, it shows how we often do things with an unthinking lack of creativity simply because we think it's the way they should be done, the way they've always been done and because that's the way everyone else would do them. In doing so, we overlook the fact that it is just as valid to do them in wholly different ways. This is at the heart of the independent thinking mindset.

Secondly, quite often the most creative of results demands the most improbable of starting points. As with escalators and fitness clubs, join at the same place as everyone else and you'll end up at the same place as everyone else, one way or another.

When it comes to independent thinking, if we simply repeat the experiences, expectations and actions of the people who went before us – parents, teachers, colleagues – then what we are saying is: 'This is as good as it gets'. We are making the statement that the only way of doing something is the way that it has been done and, although we might not say it out loud, we are quite clearly repeating the stock-in-trade response of the mundane jobsworth: 'If there was a better way then we would be doing it already'. A great example of this last creativity-killer can be found in the fascinating book *The Lighthouse Stevensons*.[1] Author Bella Bathurst points out a similar line in logic that was used by Trinity

---

1   B. Bathurst, *The Lighthouse Stevensons* (London: Harper Perennial, 2005).

House, the board who were – and still are – responsible for lighthouses in the UK. In 1635, to argue why there had not been any lighthouses built around the notorious Goodwin Sands, a treacherous area of water near the mouth of the Thames and one of the most dangerous stretches to be found around the UK, they stated without irony:

'If lighthouses had been of any service (around the area in question) the Trinity House as guardians of the interests of shipping would have put them there.'

Observations

The Internet should be less the place you go to look for answers and more where you go to inform your answers.

Because we use language to create the world, so can we change the world by changing our language.

The more certain you are, the less I trust what you say.

It might encourage us to make the most of our time on earth if our age were measured as a counting down rather than a counting up, something which gives a false sense of our going on forever.

Do You Have a Philosophy of Education?

In many countries, teacher training is being wrested away from those 'Marxist hotbeds', the university teacher-training institutions, and devolved to schools and other organisations whose job it is to impart the trade of teaching. As the Texas Teachers' billboards read, 'Want to teach? When can you start?'[1]

Whilst committed educationalists were debating whether teaching is an art or a science, a new wave of educators stormed the classroom – those who know it as a trade, something you learn 'on the job'. This new wave, embodied in the likes of Teach for America, Enseña Chile and, in the UK, Teach First, are like any group of new teachers – committed, intelligent, ambitious young people, some of whom will go on to be great educators and some of whom should be kept away from children with a Taser.

What I am increasingly convinced of, though, is the need for all teachers to have reflected deeply about, identified and committed fully to their own 'philosophy of education'. That is to say, the higher guiding purpose that they strongly believe lies behind what the day-to-day job is all about. A philosophy of education

---

1 According to an article in the *New York Times*, in May 2011, for just US$4,195 and with the option of 'fully online instruction', you can become a teacher after a few hours.

is what you would shout if I were to wake you in the middle of the night and demand to know 'What's the point of school?'

I find that if you scratch the surface of many teachers they fall into two camps – those who came into teaching because their time at school as a child was so great they wanted others to share that experience, and those who hated their school days so much that they were determined to come back to the world of education to put right a great wrong and ensure no one would ever again suffer in the way they did. Although either of these is valid as a motive for wanting to teach, neither could be classed as a philosophy of education.

If you are worried that you don't have a philosophy of education or, as a parent reading this, that you've never thought to ask your children's teachers what theirs is, don't worry. I have been involved in education for over 20 years and it is only in the last few years that I have truly identified mine.[2] It now determines how I act within and upon the field, from the smallest tweet to the largest keynote address, through my books, my TEDx talks and my organisation. Interestingly, tellingly, this realisation didn't come about through the actual act of teaching or even during my interactions with schools around the world. It came

---

2   It's the one I have borrowed from Paulo Freire and cite in the introduction.

from sitting quietly reading an important, often opaque, scholarly work on the practice and theory of education. Exactly the sort of practice that is becoming increasingly rare in our newly qualified teachers and their exposure to a more mechanistic – press lever A: teaching and product Z: learning will come out the other end – approach to education.

So, take the challenge. Be the one person in your school who continually asks that Golden Question: What is your philosophy of education? Ask your colleagues. Ask your school leaders. Ask your governing body. Ask the candidates who come through the door on interview. Ask your newly qualified teachers. Ask the 'experts' who show up to deliver training. Ask your local politicians. Ask anyone who is espousing a view on, an interest in or a degree of control over the world of education.

And make sure you take the time to reflect as deeply as is needed, and for as long as is necessary, to come up with your own answer to that question. At least the next time I demand you tell me what the point of school is you will be able to answer me and not just shout, 'What are you doing in my bedroom?!'

Observations

Of all forms of revenge, forgiveness is the hardest both to give and receive.

Like leadership, parenting works best when it consists
of a set of principles, not rules.

That two and two make four is a fact. That two and two always
make four is an opinion.

Knowledge is power, but without action it's just knowledge.

Slow Children

I live near a remedial school. There's a sign on the road outside that says, 'SLOW CHILDREN'. That can't be good for their self-esteem.

Jimmy Carr

The danger as a quick thinker is to end up only ever thinking quickly. Slow thinking can reveal insights that quick thinking never has the opportunity to spot. One of the most intelligent people I have ever worked with is one of the slowest thinkers I have ever met, something that is both infuriating in a business meeting but reassuring too.

Are you ensuring your learners think slowly as well as quickly? If our lessons are built on speed, the hands-up, first-past-the-post, guess-what's-in-my-head-and-I'll-throw-you-a-bone model, then not only are we excluding, to their long-term detriment, the neurological 'slow processors' of the world, we are also predisposing the future to be run by quick-witted individuals who never really get past their first response to a challenge. 'Will the first person to stop thinking put their hand up', as someone tweeted recently.

Whenever a child sits there smugly and tells you he or she has finished, simply ask them if that is their first answer or their best answer and leave them to come up with at least three more responses. Of course, if there is only one answer to the question, an answer at which they arrived with so little effort, then maybe it was the wrong question and you should be the one trying harder.

Observations

It is foolish to assume that because everyone is walking with an
umbrella then it must be raining.

The success of former independent school students in sports and the Arts is
not so much a victory for the private system as a tragedy of the state system.

Any reckoning of the achievements of an individual, an organisation or a state
should always be measured against these three words – at what cost?

When you know there are only two answers, always ask for three –
they might surprise you.

If You're Ever Thinking About Moving Abroad

Research has proven that living and working abroad improves your creativity and negotiating skills. What's more, it shows that the longer you have worked overseas, the more likely you are to be able to solve problems. As someone who has lived in Dubai, where the road on which you drove to work can have disappeared by the time you drive home, I can well understand it. Even the simplest of experiences, like asking for a short back and sides using only mime in Santiago, can make your brain hurt, but they are all experiences of the world that I wouldn't change for that world.

That said, living aboard is not for everyone. And it certainly isn't for you if you are not interested in any of the following:

Advertising

Architecture

Art

Biology

Birds

Challenge

Civilization

Commerce

Conservation

Consumerism

Culture

Dance

Design

Ecology

Economics	Medicine
Equality	Music
Exploration	People
Festivals	Plants
Food	Poverty
Government	Religion
History	Shopping
Infrastructure	Society
Insects	Thinking
Justice	Travel
Language	Trees
Linguistics	Urbanisation
Media	Zoology

If, after reading this, you still feel you would like to live and work abroad, then I feel it is important that you remember these three simple rules based on my field observations of British expats:

1. Don't wear sportswear in the street.
2. Don't wear Bermuda shorts to the mall.
3. Don't call it a mall.

On Leadership I

There are only two secrets to good leadership. One is to encourage special people to be themselves in the opportunities you give them. The other is attracting special people.

The secret of good management, it should be noted, is retaining special people.

Seek and Ye Shall Find (and Look Cleverer Than You Really Are)

I would like to think that I came up with the name 'Independent Thinking' for my fledgling company back in 1993 because it stood for everything I believed in and wanted to achieve by setting it up. If that were true, it would give the impression that I knew what I was doing, that I had a vision and that I had put together a clear plan. If only …

Looking around for a name for the company and drawing blanks at every turn, I turned to the age-old creative adage, borrowed from Matthew 7:7 – seek, and ye shall find. The answer to whatever conundrum you have is, like a naughty child on a training day, out there. You only have to look for it.

On the way back home from my teaching job, I decided that I would find inspiration for just the right name in something that I would spot on the journey. I seem to remember Reginald Perrin doing something similar when coming up with a new name after his 'disappearance' by choosing the first thing he saw when he looked over a fence, but then deciding that Colin Cowpat might not be quite right.

As is so often the case, the moment I started looking I found the answer right in front of me. We were following a yellow three-wheeled Robin Reliant and, this being the early 1990s, *Only Fools and Horses* was enjoying its run on BBC TV. It was only a small creative leap from 'Trotters Independent Traders' to 'Independent Thinking Ltd'. Although I did have to avoid 'The Independent Thinking Co.' en route.

Thunks

Would you call a doctor who refused to kill herself and donate her heart to save a patient selfish?

Are some human lives worth more than others?

Is a mirror more of a window than a door is?

Has anyone who has owned a Ferrari ever made the world a better place?

Does your height influence your personality?

Should vegetarians not listen to musicians who use strings made from animal gut on their instruments?

Is anger a better force for good than happiness?

How to Make a Difference

You have to ask yourself two questions.

Firstly, what can only I do?
Secondly, what have only I got?

In other words, what power, influence, ability, structures, ideas, potential, knowledge, contacts, support, beliefs, skills, insight, anger and love do I have that will allow me to make the difference that only I can make?

Observations

In a blog you have an effectively infinite amount of space. Please refrain from seeing that as an incentive to fill it. Neither my concentration span nor my will to live will expand commensurately.

Life is an endless stream of possibilities impeded by apathy.

Do BMW drivers behave the way they do because they own a BMW or do they own a BMW because they behave the way they do?

A hundred years from now, all that will be left of today's educationalists and the arguments they have will be the arguments.

Should We Be Teaching Children To Be Principled But Unreasonable?

George Bernard Shaw's famous quote – 'The reasonable man adapts himself to the world; the unreasonable one persists in trying to adapt the world to himself. Therefore, all progress depends on the unreasonable man' – is echoed in the work of the influential Brazilian educationalist Paulo Freire. Rather than being either reasonable or unreasonable, he suggests that our dichotomy is between being either 'adapted' or 'integrated'.[1]

The 'adapted' person is the one who is the 'object' in the sentence, who fits in, who knows his place, who doesn't cause a fuss or stand out in any way. He or she adapts to the pressures and expectations, to his or her lot.

Among the staff at school, they make good seconds in department.

Among the students, they make good prefects.

'Integrated' individuals differ from adapted ones in two key aspects, according to Freire. When faced with the same reality confronting the adapted ones, integrated individuals reveal 'the critical capacity to make choices' combined with the intent and the power 'to transform that reality'.

---

1   P. Freire, *Education for Critical Consciousness* (London: Continuum, 1974).

Among the staff, they are often school leaders. But not always.

Among the students, they are often in detention. As Freire says, 'Unpliant men with a revolutionary spirit are often termed "maladjusted".'

My own short-hand for this dichotomous understanding of the differences between the movers and shakers and the sitters and tremblers is what I have elsewhere referred to as DDMs and DMDs. The former group are the 'Don't Do; Moans'; the latter group are the 'Don't Moan; Dos'. A quick check in the staffroom will reveal who is in what camp.

Look at the spirit of the individuals in your classes, of the children who come into contact with you on a regular basis, at the culture and ethos being perpetrated throughout your organisation, and then ask yourself three questions:

1. Are we teaching our children to adapt or integrate?
2. What will happen when these young people are running the world?
3. Can I sleep at night?

On Control

I have my least favourite and my most favourite pieces of music on my iPod. Whenever either of them comes on, I switch them off immediately.

In the case of my most favourite piece, I don't want to wear it out. I want to choose how and when I will enjoy it and I have probably listened to it not more than twice in the last four years.

In the case of my least favourite track, whenever it comes on as I shuffle through my music, I take the greatest of delights in letting the intro play and then, just as the vocals are about to kick in, hitting the skip button.

It's a control thing that was impossible when all you had was the radio.

Observations

A school is never as good as its head teacher says it is, but it is always better than its teachers claim it to be.

Happy endings are only verifiable in hindsight.

When it comes to the dumbing down of the teaching profession, it is worth remembering that owning a bag of spanners doesn't make you a plumber.

There is no such thing as 'cope'.

And What Do You Do?

Just think, if I had followed my careers advice I could have been an accountant by now.

I'm not sure what advice you are sharing with young people about their future careers (other than the dubious 'work hard and you'll go far' non sequitur), but I'm sure it won't involve any of the jobs listed below, all of which are real and many of which are surprisingly well paid.

That said, the more we can encourage young people that it's not about the money, the better. The British philosopher Alan Watts used to ask students what it was they would really like to do 'if money were no object'. Many replied that they would like to be poets or painters or writers, but they usually added, 'But you can't earn any money that way'. To this Watts had this to say:

> *Forget the money, because, if you say that getting the money is the most important thing, you will spend your life completely wasting your time. You'll be doing things you don't like doing in order to go on living, that is to go on doing things you don't like doing, which is stupid. Better to have a short life that is full of what you like doing than a long life spent in a miserable way.*[1]

---

1   Alan Watts, 'What If Money Were No Object?', YouTube. Available at www.youtube.com/watch?v=45kNqUF6kC4 (accessed 12 August 2013).

What would you be doing now if you had followed this advice? Who knows, maybe you could have ended up an ethical hacker or a Lego sculptor …

Aeroplane repo man	Desert island caretaker
Animal colourist	Dog babysitter
Artificial insemination technician	Dog yoga teacher
Banana gasser	Doll fashion designer
Bed bug host	Embalmer
Beer taster	Ethical computer hacker
Bounty hunter	Face feeler
Brewmaster	Female social drinker
Cat behaviour consultant	Flavour chemist
Cat holder-downer	Forest fire lookout
Chief listening officer	Fortune cookie writer
Chocolate consultant	Furniture tester
Citrus fruit dyer	Futurist
Clinical ethicist	Global mobility consultant
Computational linguist	Golf ball diver
Crime scene cleaner	Gorilla
Custom implant organ designer	Greeting card writer
Data scientist	Hair boiler

Hair simulation supervisor

Horse exerciser

Ice-cream taster

Laughter therapist

Lego sculptor

Light bender

Luxury house-sitter

Monkey trainer

Nanotechnologist

Nasty stunt producer

Nude cruise worker

Ocularist

Osteo-archaeologist

Oyster floater

Pancake flipper

Paper towel sniffer

Penguinologist

Pet food taster

Placenta cook

Poison taster

Pornography historian

Professional granny

Professional queuer

Professional sleeper

Prosthetist

Psychic

Shark tagger

Shark tank cleaner

Snake milker

Stand-in bridesmaid

Submarine cook

Technical lingerie model

Teddy bear repair technician

Teen exorcist

Tequila shot girl

Trivia writer

TV caption writer

TV corpse

UFO desk officer

Urine drug screen collector

Voice-over artist

Water listener

Waterslide tester

Webcam model

Weed farmer

Wrinkle chaser[2]

It was hard enough to 'follow your dreams' after leaving education before, but now, saddled with tens of thousands of pounds worth of student debt, there is even less incentive to try something risky but exciting with your life and even more pressure to join the rat race to service the debt and accrue more on the way. In other words, you get the best education you can because they tell you it will help you get the best job you can, and then you take the first job that comes along because you need a salary to pay for the education that you received in order to get what you thought would be a better job.

As Watts says, in his inimitable style:

> We're bringing up children and educating them to live the same sort of lives we are living in order that they may justify themselves and find satisfaction in life by bringing up their children to bring up their children to do the same thing. So it's all retch, and no vomit. It never gets there.[3]

---

2 Sources: www.money.aol.co.uk, www.admastblog.co.uk, www.dailyfinance.com, www.crocktock.com, www.techi.com, www.yahoo.com, www.listal.com, www.coburgbanks.co.uk, www.totaljobs.com, www.mandatory.com, www.forbes.com, www.salary.com, www.theuncagedlife.com, www.msn.com, www.cnbc.com, www.brazencareerist.com, www.bbc.co.uk, www.aol.com, www.markconner.typepad.com.

3 Watts, 'What If Money Were No Object?'

Observations

I dread disappointment more than I do death although, knowing my luck,
I'll live forever.

Without plans, the illness is all you have.

The first nation to create an educational assessment tool fit for purpose in the
21st century will be the one that wins.

Are you the thing or the image of the thing?

Learning is Overrated

I was having a Friday night beer with a friend in a Cuban bar in Hong Kong, sitting under a violent air conditioning unit and watching the street cats hover hungrily behind the baobab trees.

He told me how, as a teacher who was trained in craft, design and technology, he felt that the subject should actually be part of the humanities department. Done properly, it's not about making things and 'learning how to do a butt joint'. It's about understanding what's wrong in the world and then creating something physical that can serve to make that problem go away.

His subject is, thus, the outward physical response to an intellectual, empathetic, socially driven stimulus.

It resonated with a discussion I'd had with another teacher of the subject not that long before. He had put forward a paper to his department arguing the case for less 'teaching children how to build clocks' and more 'exploring the nature of time, the way it is used and the ways in which it is portrayed'. 'Half of my department', he told me, 'thought it was great. The other half wanted to burn me at the stake.'

I have been in too many lessons where the children are learning *to do* something – differential equations, conjugate an irregular verb, butt joints – but have no idea why they are learning this and certainly no engagement with a greater purpose to motivate this learning. Despite the fact that they were all learning, often learning well, and may well go on to achieve top grades in their exams, there was still the elephant in the room sitting on the workbench – what was achieved here, really?

If the focus of our lessons, or at least the initial premise, is one related to thinking, then we are never wasting time, theirs or ours. If our woodwork lesson is linked to a greater, higher purpose then my butt joint may not be as good as your butt joint, and I may never cut it as a full-time carpenter (if you pardon the pun), but at least I will have come to understand something important about the world, the way it is and the people in it. And, if that is combined with an understanding of myself and the things that I am good at, then I can work to solve the same sorts of problems but in a way that suits me better.

In her glorious teacher's bible *Full On Learning*,[1] Zoë Elder uses the line, 'Before you build a boat you have to need a boat'. In other words, any great physical achievement has to be motivated by a physical need experienced in an intellectual way. To build a better itch-scratcher you not only need an itch

---

1 Z. Elder, *Full On Learning: Involve Me and I'll Understand* (Carmarthen: Crown House Publishing, 2012).

but you also need to want to scratch that itch in a way that it has never been scratched before.

If all you do is concentrate on the learning – whether it's done by rote, at one extreme, or problem-based enquiry at the other, whether it's micro-managed with a Hattie-esque fervour or you take the more hands-off approach in a laissez-faire Sugata Mitra style, or anywhere in-between – at the end, all you will have is the learning. Nothing has changed. What was once learned elsewhere has been learned again here. Like a rapidly multiplying virus, you have simply infected more people with 'stuff' which, under the microscope, is a carbon-copy replica of the same stuff in the heads of thousands of children up and down the country and which will be extracted during a 'routine examination' and sent away to the exam board for analysis like sputum in a phial.

If learning is what is needed, let them learn, but only as a personal and intellectual response to a real-world problem, the first steps of which involve reflection, contemplation, empathy, understanding and problem spotting as well as solving. In this way, the outcomes of this learning can be measured in more ways than just exam success; you are also preparing young people to change the world for the better, one butt joint at a time.

On Grief

Grief brings with it a great drawing in, a closing down. There is no tomorrow. Today is a succession of moments. You do not move through time. You stand still, unmoving, as if on a beach, and wave upon wave of emotion rolls in upon you relentlessly. You cannot hide or turn from these waves. You cannot anticipate when the next one will suddenly appear. Waves only break in the final part of their journey, after all. Suddenly, one is upon you. Then, depending on the wave, you cry or you rant or you plead or you rail or you howl or you sigh or you draw your hand to your mouth and gasp for air, for life, uncontrollably, as your eyes dart about the room searching desperately for something solid, reassuring, that will hold you up, hold you back, tell you that life is how it was. Except it will never be how it was.

But this is a realisation that creeps over you slowly.

But now, for now, is all you have. You glimpse at the future – When will I work again? When do I need to go shopping? What bureaucracies do I need to inform of the death? – all the tittle-tattle of diurnal life, but then draw back in, unmotivated and desolate, knowing there is no future. Or, at least, not one that counts. There is just now. Each of us on our beach, staring disconsolately at a horizon that seems so sad, buffeted by the waves.

The Serendipitous Benefits of Bad Taxi Drivers

If ever you get into a taxi and they mistakenly take you to the wrong place, don't get cross – get out of the taxi anyway. There may well be a reason they took you to this place that neither you nor they will ever know unless you look.

This has now happened to me twice – interestingly, both times leaving the same London hotel.

With aeroplane travel, this is a more hazardous approach due to visa restrictions and issues of immunisation.

How to Know Whether You're a Humanist or a Scientist

When you're crossing the river you look at the view.

You have a pencil case full of different colour pens, many of which don't work.

Your watch has two functions.

You buy Apple because of how it looks.

You choose a new car based on its colour.

The display on your DVD player is still flashing.

Your friends come to you with their personal problems.

When you're in the garden you marvel at the roses.

When you're crossing the river you look at the bridge.

You have two pens, both black. And a red one. In case you have to annotate unexpectedly.

Your watch can tell you the time on Venus.

You buy Apple because of how it performs.

You choose a new car based on its particulate emissions.

The display on your answer phone never flashes.

Your friends come to you with their technical problems.

When you're in the garden you marvel at the irrigation system.

When you meet a stranger you ask them what inspires them.

You don't meet strangers.

You see an equation as a thing of beauty.

You see a thing of beauty as an equation.

Your closest friends are the ones you're with at the time.

Your closest friends are the ones you know only through Facebook.

When you see rainbows you think about dreams.

When you see rainbows you think about prisms.

When you see a crippled beggar you think about how to help them.

When you see a crippled beggar you think about how to heal them.

When looking at the stars you wish you had a blanket.

When looking at the stars you wish you had a telescope.

You like the smile of the server behind the delicatessen counter in the supermarket.

You shop online. Mainly pizza.

Your CDs aren't arranged in alphabetical order.

Your music is on a one-terabyte external drive. Mainly Pink Floyd.

You keep telling people that one day you'll write a novel.

You keep telling people that one day you'll read a novel.

You appreciate that love is a question of chemistry.

You appreciate that everything is a question of chemistry.

Observations

Without a knowledge of history, you catch sight of the pendulum swinging and mistake it for an entire revolution.

Some people in an organisation are like conifers in that they give an impression of structure but drain far more from their surroundings than they put back in.

'Can I go on?' is always a rhetorical question. Onwards is the only direction over which you have no choice.

It is a little-known fact that Beethoven is the only composer whose work can always be heard over the sound of the ocean, no matter how softly you play it.

It's Not Succeeding That's Hard, It's Keeping Going

Despite what they portray in the films, there is no such thing as a happy ending. It's a decision you can only make in hindsight, by which time it's too late. After all, achieving something significant, although hard, isn't the hardest part. It's the keeping going that hurts. It's like trail running. Reaching the summit of a steep hill nearly kills you, but you know you can make it if you just put one foot in front of the other enough times. It's what happens when you get to the top that determines what sort of person you are, though. Collapse in a self-congratulatory heap or keep going?

Or, put another way, compare the ongoing rise of Madonna:

1985 – The Virgin Tour – grossed US$5 million

1987 – The Who's That Girl Tour – grossed US$25 million

1990 – The Blond Ambition Tour – grossed US$60 mllion

1993 – The Girlie Show – grossed US$70 million

2001 – The Drowned World Tour – grossed US$75 million

2004 – The Re-Invention World Tour – grossed US$125 million

2006 – The Confessions Tour – grossed US$194.7 million

2008 – The Sweet and Sticky Tour – grossed US$282 million

2012 – The MDNA Tour – grossed US$305 million

with the descent into the depths of the *Jaws* franchise:

1975 – *Jaws 1* – Grossed US$470,653,000

1978 – *Jaws 2* – Grossed US$187,884,000

1983 – *Jaws 3-D* – Grossed US$87,987,055

1987 – *Jaws 4: The Revenge* – Grossed US$51,881,013[1]

When it comes to success, you just have to pick yourself up and keep going.

---

1   All figures courtesy of Wikipedia as of 12 August 2013.

Circumspice

In the eye,
Where the globe's
Reflected jets ponder,
Of the crow
On the back
Of the cow
In a field
Near the path
By the boat-bitten river
Near the park
On a hill
Where the deer
Dandle twitching
By the mount
Of a king
Near a hedge
With a space
Where your eye

Simply tears
Unencumbered
Through the city,
Bristling chimneys,
Of the blind
In the haze
On a hint-
Of-spring
Day
To the sight
Barely there
Of the dome
Ris'n to God
Where the man
Asked his gift
Simply said
Arms outspread
With a cry

'Look around'
Is the world
When you look,
If you look,
The crow on
The back of
The cow
In the eye.

Written in Petersham Meadows, by the Thames, London

Thunks

Does a dog mind what you stroke it with?

Is the sole goal behind educating poor people that they stop being poor?

Are schools democratic?

Can you be a head teacher if you've never been a teacher and can you be a good head teacher if you've never been a good teacher?

If you bully someone but the person you bully doesn't know you're bullying them, is it still bullying?

Is cynicism the opposite of optimism more than pessimism is?

Could you have a pet tree? If you did, could you ever teach it to 'stay' and if you called it to 'Come!', and it didn't, would it be misbehaving?

On Finding Things

Often, it is when you are not looking for things that you find them. I once saw a crab floating in the middle of the sea on a ferry trip in Brittany. If I had gone looking for a floating crab in the middle of the sea around Brittany, there is very little chance I would have found it but, by not looking for it, there it was.

I started applying that 'don't seek and ye shall' find mentality in day-to-day life, and it works. Once I was fruitlessly looking for a fishing tackle shop with my son in the backstreets of Ipswich. After half an hour we decided to look for an Indian restaurant instead. We found the fishing tackle shop within minutes.

Once I dropped the valve cap from the tyre I was inflating in a garage in Wales. After a few minutes looking for it without success, I decided the best way to find it was to stop looking for it. I found it almost immediately.

When you're at sea, at night, the best way to see a very faint light is not to look at it. It's the same with stars. We have stronger vision from the sides of our eyes than full on.

The question is, what else can we find by not looking for it and what else can we see by not looking at it?

How to Get a Job

In the old days it would be after a conference address or a training day. A teacher who had been in the audience would come up and tell me that they could do what I do and could they join my company. My response would always consist of three steps:

1. Pat myself silently on the back for having made it look easy.

2. Question them to see if their motive for no longer wanting to be a teacher was one driven by moving away or moving towards. Wanting to do something is a very different motivator from not wanting to do something. In the former, you are driven by the sort of self-belief and moral purpose that will see you through the bad times. In the latter, you will race towards any port in the storm.

3. Give them a business card and ask them to get in touch to let me know what they would 'bring to the party'. Asking someone to actually take action about something is the single biggest way I have found of eliminating 99% of the people in this situation. It's not my job to give you a job with me. It's yours. What are you going to do about it?

Short Story

A man went to the zoo to see the animals. He found himself looking through the bars at a lion. 'What's it like to live your days in a cage?' asked the lion.

The man went to the park to look at the king's sculptures. He found himself standing before a statue. 'What's it like to do the same thing day after day?' asked the statue.

Then he went to the hospital to visit the sick. He found himself standing by the bed of a dying child. 'I wish there was something I could do to cheer you up,' said the child.

Whose Problem is the Future and the 100-Year Plan?

I once read that politicians should be forced to make decisions based on the effects those decisions would have upon their children's children's children. In other words, that they do nothing for short-term personal gain and everything in the longer-term interests of the world as a whole.

To achieve this would take a 100-year plan.

Humans, by design, have a very short-term view of things. We are wired up to see changing but not change. We see the tide come in; we see the tide go out. Yet it's hard to observe the tide going in and out. We can spot the danger of a car veering towards us, but not the threat to our children's children's children of what a billion cars are doing to the planet, or what Plan B might be and how we could embark on it now so things will be improved by the time the earth is in their hands.

If it wanted to, the education system could change that. And I mean really change it, not just run the occasional Green Week or organise a human school bus every now and again. While those activities have their place, they are not getting to the root of the opportunity thrown up by mega-problems, that is to say mega-thinking and, equally, mega-involvement. To what extent are we inculcating children with a spirit of participation in the process of making things better? To what extent are we teaching children about the world in order that they feel motivated, empowered and expected to improve the world?

If we had brave politicians they would put together a 100-year plan, not one that simply lasted long enough to see them through to the next hustings. In China they have a 10-year plan for education. Even that is a start. A 100-year plan would allow us to introduce policies that genuinely moved humanity in the right direction. But if we wait for politicians to put together a 100-year plan, we might be waiting for, well, 100 years. Start it now. What do your children want 2113 to look like and what will they do today to move towards it? Now that's what I call a homework assignment.

The Thing About Shelves

I

If you only ever look for off-the-shelf solutions then how good you become will be forever limited by the size of your shelf.

II

I have been in many a school leader's office and seen their bookshelves full of the latest literature on education and leadership, most of it in pristine condition. In fact, the only book that ever looks like it's been well read is the one on instant assembly ideas for all occasions.

Maybe the following three-point plan for book shelves might help:

1. If you have a book but don't read it within three months, give it to someone else.
2. Once you have read it give it to someone else.

3. Only keep the books that are dog-eared with use and peppered with sticky notes and highlighter pen marks. Put them on a long piece of string and attach them to your shelf.

III

When it comes to government documents and circulations from on high, one head teacher I met used the following six-point shelf-related prioritisation strategy:

4. Put up a single shelf along one wall.
5. Under the shelf at one end put a bin.
6. Add new documents and ring-binder folders to the shelf on the end furthest from the bin.
7. Use the bin to catch the oldest folders and documents that are displaced from the shelf by the new arrivals.
8. Recycle.
9. Repeat ad nauseum.

One Little Girl's Story[1]

The little girl was sad. She was halfway through the school year and, although she was trying really hard, she was so scared of the teacher (who shouted a lot if the little girl didn't understand things) that she was going to do badly in her end-of-year tests and was going to have to repeat the school year. More trying hard. More shouting. She was very sad indeed.

She decided she was going to ask her parents to help her. Maybe her father, who she knew worked hard from sun to sun, could drink a little less when he was home and maybe help her with her schoolwork a little more. And maybe her mother could help her too, although she knew she had her other brothers and sisters to look after now, especially the very young ones, and the new baby was on its way. When she did pluck up the courage to ask her parents, all they could do was shrug their shoulders and tell her that she should try harder at school and that it was up to her teacher to help her learn. It wasn't their fault.

Determined to try harder, she went to her teacher and told her that she really didn't want to repeat the last year and that she had tried very hard to learn. It was just all the shouting had really frightened her and was there anything the teacher could do to help her. The teacher looked down her glasses at the girl, smiled in way that wasn't really a smile at all, and told her she had 40 other

---

1   Although this is a fictional story, it is an amalgam of true events drawn from my time observing the free-market, neo-liberal, looking-glass world of the Chilean educational system.

children to help in class and if the little girl didn't learn what she was teaching her then what was she supposed to do about it. She added: 'If you're not clever enough to do well in my lessons then it's hardly my fault, is it?'

The little girl felt very unhappy about this answer (although she didn't know why) and so she summoned up all her courage and went and knocked on the door of the school's head teacher. This was a woman that she didn't see very often, apart from on Mondays when they had to sing the national anthem very loudly outside in the dusty square in the middle of the school. She had a fierce face and always looked like she wished she was someone else. The fierce face met the little girl as she was ushered into the office by the old lady who always sat outside, and it listened with growing impatience as the little girl explained that she really didn't want to repeat a year and was there anything the head teacher could do to help her as she really was trying very hard.

There was a man with a beard sitting on an old wooden chair in one corner of the head teacher's office copying information from the School Book (where the little girl's name was written each time she was late or had been naughty or had not been able to come to school as her mother had needed her to help with the little ones as she was in bed or drunk). The head teacher raised her hand to stop the girl talking and pointed out that she ran the best school she could with the money they gave her (the little girl noticed that the head teacher pointed with her thin lips in the direction of the man with the beard sitting in the corner when she said the word 'they') and that maybe the girl should have paid more attention to what her teacher was saying in class and that having to repeat a year wasn't her fault.

Just as she was about to leave, the man with the beard lifted his head from the Book and told her, with a smile aimed not at the girl but at the head teacher, that the little girl should go and speak to the Mayor if she wasn't happy with her school. The little girl thanked him for his suggestion (although she wasn't really sure what a 'Mayor' was), apologised for disturbing the head teacher and the man with the beard and left the room.

The Mayor was a fat man with a shiny forehead and a handkerchief in his hand with which he dabbed at his face without knowing he was doing it. He was not used to having children in his office and was looking at the little girl rather warily, his eyes flicking between her face and a small black-and-white photo he had on his desk of an old man with white hair wearing the uniform of an important general. The general was smiling. The girl simply explained that she had tried very hard this year and that she didn't want to repeat a year, but that her teacher kept shouting at her when she didn't understand and that this was really not very helpful to her.

'Ah, well,' said the Mayor, looking relieved, 'the problem is that the teachers we get here have not been trained properly by the universities.' He suggested that she go and speak to all the very many experts who worked at the teacher-training universities and see what they had to say about the matter because, after all, 'The quality of teachers is hardly my fault.'

The girl thanked the Mayor for his time and wondered what a 'university' was.

Eventually she found some universities, after a quite a long bus ride that took her far from her end of town. Quite a few of them had writing all over the walls

123

and noisy groups of young people outside shouting and waving big flags, and the girl was frightened by the big green vans that were squirting water and the strange smell that made her cry. Eventually, though, after she had travelled even further from her home, she found one with no angry people outside. It was a large building with bright posters telling everyone how good it was. The little girl thought that everybody going in and out looked very important.

She found the place where the people who trained teachers were based and asked a nicely dressed lady, who had the words 'Director of Faculty' on her desk, who she could talk to about helping teachers be better. The nice lady said that that having better teachers wasn't really very practical and, anyway, it wasn't her job, but she would introduce her to a man called 'the Dean' who had responsibility for making sure that teachers knew how best to help little boys and girls learn.

The Dean was a kindly man with a smiley face who listened patiently to the little girl's story. He even arranged for the lady with the nice clothes to bring the little girl some juice and biscuits. When she had finished, the Dean gave the girl a lovely smile and told her that he fully understood her concerns. He told her that he wasn't a teacher and had never been a teacher (although he did own a school or two) but that he had so many wonderful plans to ensure that all the little girls and boys across the land would be taught by wonderful teachers in the future. When she heard this the little girl smiled happily. 'But,' said the Dean (at which point the girl's smile started to fade), 'the man who owns the university is keeping too much of the money he is making and that means I can't make all the teachers as wonderful as I had planned to do. In fact, the most I can do is to make sure all the student teachers graduate, even if they're not very good.'

He then went on to use big words that the little girl had never heard before, like 'accreditation' and 'budgetary pressures' and 'key performance indicators', before telling her that the biggest reason he couldn't make all his wonderful plans come true was because of the 'Ministry', which really wasn't that interested in making teachers better. Offering her another biscuit, he suggested she go to see some people in a building on a hill looking out across the mountains and that it was up to them to make teachers better. He stood up (so she knew her time with this man was over) and, as she was leaving, he apologised very nicely and told her that he took full responsibility for the fact that teachers not being better wasn't his fault.

The big building on the hill was as far away from the little girl's end of town as she could possibly go (although she did have an aunt who lived in a wooden house on a hill nearby that looked out across the school where the shiny American children go and every classroom is full of apples, or so she had been told). She walked up the big steps as the eagles circled high overhead and hummingbirds danced in the gardens and where the air seemed so much cleaner than she had ever breathed before. A lady met her in an office that was full of folders and piles of paper and who had the same busy, important face that all the other people she had met had too. She listened to the little girl's story, only looking at her watch once or twice, and repeatedly shifted a large pile of papers from one side of her desk to another.

When the little girl had finished the lady gave the girl a sort-of smile and pointed out that, of course, the little girl's teacher should be better and that it was terrible that so many teachers and head teachers and schools were so bad, and that she was doing everything she could do to make them like the wonderful schools that lay over the mountains, and that she always listened very carefully to all the visiting professors who came so often to the country to talk for a day about what should be done, but that, really, it was so hard to make changes with so much paperwork to do and so many people (and here the little girl thinks she used the word 'donkeys' but she couldn't be sure) simply not doing their job properly, and so she was very sorry but she had a meeting to go to and maybe she should go and see the nice man in charge ('at the moment') of all of the teachers in the land as it really wasn't her fault.

The little girl took a bus from the building with the hummingbirds and the clean air and the mountains back to the middle of the city to a building with a big metal gate and a scary shield above it that said 'Force or Reason'. She approached a friendly lady at the reception desk and asked to see the man in charge of teachers for all the land. The lady seemed to smile to herself and said something like she would 'check who it was today'. She then sent the girl up in the lift to the top floor and, just as she was stepping out of the lift, a harassed-looking man in a dark suit pushed past her, got into the lift and jabbed impatiently at the button for it to go back down. He was carrying his coat in one hand and talking into his mobile phone, saying something about needing to spend more time with his family and that 'it's not my fault anyway'.

The little girl watched the lift door close, then turned and walked nervously towards a heavy wooden door with the word 'Minister of Education' on it. The man had left it slightly ajar in his hurry to leave and so the girl pushed it gingerly. It swung open to reveal an empty room with shining wooden walls and a big wooden desk with a green leather top. On the wall behind it was a picture of an important-looking person wearing what looked like a flag. Although the important person's face looked vaguely familiar, the little girl didn't quite know who it was or what that person did. She noticed that the very important person was smiling and looking very pleased, as if something significant had been achieved.

Observations

We could argue that the bankers should only get their bonuses once they've helped us to achieve world peace but the trouble is, after we've achieved world peace, their bonuses would be a lot smaller.

Good head teachers make things happen. Good deputies make sure things happen.

If you have money and power, the thing you want above all else is money and power.

I refuse to let your evidence as to why something won't work get in the way of my making it work.

The Difference Between Creativity and Art

Creativity is *when*.

Art is *now*.

It is impossible to 'do' art effectively if you're not able to be in the now.

The Cure

Every morning he was there, the mad man, on the corner of the street, talking out loud to the small voices that were both in his head yet far away. The passers-by would cross the road rather than walk past him, to avoid him, for fear of him, for fear of what he stood for.

One day a wise man saw this and knew, in his heart and without hesitation, that he could cure this poor unfortunate. Reaching inside his coat pocket, rather than crossing the street, he approached the mad man.

The following day, even though the man was still on the corner, even though he still spoke loudly to the voices that were both in his head yet far away, this time the passers-by did not cross the road to avoid him, did not turn their back on him, did not fear him. They simply walked past him as if he were not there, as if he were one of them.

On the mad man's right ear could be seen a Bluetooth headset.

Careers Advice for Young People

You can divide the world into five groups:

1. Those that create the system.
2. Those that work the system.
3. Those that serve the system.
4. Those that break the system.
5. Those that change the system.

You just have to work out where you want to be.

Observations

The top of the beer is always so much better than the bottom. It holds a promise that that the bottom knows is rarely delivered.

You can't do politics alone. It's a process of dialogue.
And dialogue on one's own is as fertile as sex on one's own.
Nor should either be discussed over dinner.

You can do what you want with facts. It's the truth that counts.

Teachers – some of your students will do well in life and others less so. You can make a difference but the gods will decide which is which.

Her Conversation with the Social Workers

'I'm sick', she said.

'When did he do this to you?' they said.

'Help me', she said.

'Yes, we must protect you', they said.

'It hurts', she said.

'Where did he hit you?' they said.

'Help me', again she said.

'Poor you!' they all said.

'I don't know if I can go on', she said.

'We'll stop him', they said.

'*Please listen to me when I beg you not to
listen to me*', she said.

'Yes, we'll protect you from him', they said.
'Monday to Friday, nine to five'.

'*Is it time*', she asked like a child, '*for me to
go home yet?*'

'You're safe now', they said. 'You have no home'.

'*Yet can I see my children?*' she asked.

'You're safe now', they said. 'He can't hurt you'.

'*But I'm loved*', she said.

'When did he do this to you?' they said.

On the Purpose of Reading

When you start reading, you read for ideas.

Then you read to have your own ideas confirmed.

Then you read to have your own ideas informed.

Then you read to have your ideas strengthened.

Then you read to have your ideas challenged.

Then you don't read.

Then you start again.

Observations

Whenever you say 'How *are* you?' to someone with a long-term illness,
remember to say 'How are *you?*' to the person by their side.

Giving is not the same as serving.

No matter how hard I try, I still can't shake off the feeling that
the great tit should be setting the blue tit an example.

To compromise, you must leave your dreams undisturbed in your head.

The Difference is the Size of the 'P'

Small groups of persons can, and do, make the rest of us think what they please about a given subject.

Edward Bernays

A question that I was never asked when I was training to be a teacher is this one: 'Should we keep politics out of the classroom?'

If I had been asked I would have indubitably said 'no'. Let children be children and save the world of greasy pole climbing and hypocritical equivocation for when they are grown up. Or at least confine it to the staffroom.

However, looking at things now, I think a far better answer would be, 'Well, that depends. Do you mean "politics" or "Politics"?'

If, by 'Politics', we are referring to party politics and the process of encouraging children to take a stance somewhere along a left–right axis then no, keep away. There is too much room for indoctrination and bias either at a conscious or an unconscious level. Children are impressionable and we should treat this preciously naïve state with the respect and care it deserves.

However, if we are talking about 'politics', that is to say, an understanding of individual, society and the state and the interactions between the three, then I am increasingly of a mind not only that we should but we must. In fact, it could be argued that sending them out into the world without such an understanding is playing right into 'their' hands.

The 'father of public relations' was a man called Edward Bernays who, in 1928, wrote the essential book for anyone studying the manipulation of the public mind for commercial or political benefit, *Propaganda*. The quote at the top of this chapter comes from this book, which he opens with the following assertion:

> *The conscious and intelligent manipulation of the organized habits and opinions of the masses is an important element in democratic society. Those who manipulate this unseen mechanism of society constitute an invisible government which is the true ruling power of our country.*[1]

Bernays was one of the first to look at selling, marketing and the subtle art of persuasion with the eye of a psychologist. He was, for example, a fan of the works of Sigmund Freud. He was also interested in the lessons that could be learned from group psychology and the ideas of, among others, the English surgeon Wilfred Trotter and his book *Instincts of the Herd in Peace and War*[2] (in which it is suggested 'how dangerous it would be to breed man for reason').

---

1   E. Bernays, *Propaganda* (New York: Horace Liveright, 1928), quoted in N. Chomsky, *Profit Over People: Neoliberalism and Global Order* (New York: Seven Stories Press, 1999).

2   W. Trotter, *Instincts of the Herd in Peace and War* (New York: MacMillan, 1919).

In particular, Bernays was interested in how 'the few' – 'a trifling fraction of our hundred and twenty million' – could manipulate 'the many':

> If we understand the mechanism and motives of the group mind, is it not possible to control and regiment the masses according to our will without their knowing it?

Now, I am not so naïve as to think that persuasion in all its various guises is always the devil's work. Life is a string of choices held together by advertising and fuelled by human frailties. I'm writing this chapter on a top-of-the-range 13" MacBook Pro with Retina display. Why? I don't know. I don't even know what a 'Retina display' is. It just makes me feel good – shallow, pathetic, middle-aged man with a credit card that I am. But it was a choice. My choice. I was aware I was being manipulated and was a willing participant.

But what about the manipulation that comes under the radar or works on us when we are too young or when our ideas not well formed enough to spot it, let alone analyse it? What about when it doesn't deal with consumerism but citizenship? Or worse, replaces citizenship with consumerism? And should we be all the more wary of that at a time when the corporate takeover of public education is in full swing? For example, according to *Education Week*, education giant Pearson has spent over US$6 million in recent years lobbying in the United States alone, the same article citing the not-for-profit 'advocacy' Foundation for Excellence in Education, which is 'working on behalf of various educational companies promoting online education policies and model bills and making connections to policymakers for its financial supporters, which include such companies as Amplify, Charter Schools USA, K12 Inc., McGraw-Hill Education, Microsoft, and Pearson Education.'[3]

(Apropos of everything and nothing, Amplify is part of Rupert Murdoch's empire, K12 Inc. is 'a publicly traded company with $708 million in revenue in 2012' and '39 lobbyists around the country on the payroll' and the Foundation for Excellence in Education was set up by Jeb Bush, one of the few members of the Bush family who hasn't yet been president.[4])

So, should we politicise the classroom in the 21st century? Only if we feel questions such as these are worthy of debate with young people:

How is the world organised and is it done so in the best possible way?

What is wrong with the world and what can be done to change it?

What is right about the world and what can be done to preserve it?

Who are the people in charge of the world and are they doing a good job?

Who will be the next generation of people running the world? Will they be the right people for the job and do I want to be part of them?

If there is something wrong, can I do anything to put it right and, if so, where do I start?

Beyond myself and my family, whose responsibility am I?

---

3   M. R. Davis, 'Ed. Companies Exert Public-Policy Influence', *Education Week*, 22 April 2013. Available at: www.edweek.org/ew/articles/2013/04/24/29ii-politicalpower.h32.html (accessed 12 August 2013).

4   Ibid.

Beyond myself and my family, what responsibilities do I hold?

Are my rights the same as your rights?

Am I in a position where I can make decisions about important things?

Am I getting the information I need to make those decisions?

Am I prepared to make those decisions and then abide by them?

How can I find out whether what 'they' are telling me is the way it really is?

What can I do about it if I find it isn't?

Can I trust you?

Should I choose to trust you even if I can?

Declining to teach children about politics for fear of turning them into Lefties or Tories, or whatever political polarisation is current, is like not teaching them French for fear of turning them, well, French. Do it because it is important. And what is equally important is to do it well.

Going back to our old friend Freire and his practice of enlisting education to generate critical consciousness, or *conscientização*, he cites the example of a Brazilian public figure in the 1960s whose publicity consisted of a bust of his likeness with various arrows pointing to the head, eyes, mouth and hands. The arrows were marked as follows:

You don't need to think, he thinks for you!

You don't need to see, he sees for you!

You don't need to talk, he talks for you!

You don't need to act, he acts for you![5]

Of course, that would never happen here ...

---

5   Freire, *Education for Critical Consciousness*.

A Real-World
Six-Point Noise Scale

1. Library voice.
2. Classroom voice.
3. Playground voice.
4. Whale song.
5. Pneumatic drill.
6. Americans speaking in a restaurant.

Observations

Life is too short to reverse into parking spaces.

I defend to the death your right to disagree with me online, but I will block you in an instant if you do it in the manner of the school bully.

What if we were to think of school as a network not a building?

The best Finnish education system is the one in Finland.

The Eight Stages of Manhood

1. In your 20s you identify who you are.

2. In your 30s you create who you are.

3. In your 40s you consolidate who you are. Or buy a sports car and go back to stage 2.

4. In your 50s you enjoy who you are.

5. In your 60s you regret who you weren't.

6. In your 70s you start to think about who you were.

7. In your 80s you start to forget who you were.

8. In your 90s you either don't know who you are or don't care as long as they'll let you watch *Countdown*.

On Value

It's not what something is – it's what we think it is that counts.

I met an antiques dealer once who told me that if an item didn't sell, she simply kept putting up the price until it did.

I also met a neighbour who used to sell second-hand furniture by leaving it outside his house. If he put up a sign that said 'Free – help yourself' nothing ever moved. If he put a price on it, he would sell it quickly.

People don't value what they don't pay for. They think they do and they think they would love for you to give them something for nothing. But they don't.

In London, I once watched newspaper vendors outside a busy Tube station. One was selling an evening newspaper. One was giving their paper away. When people took a free copy they never said thank you. When they bought one they always did.

What value are we putting on ourselves and how are we transmitting that value? Research on bullying in schools shows that children who use self-deprecating humour are more likely to be bullied than children who simply tell jokes. How much do you have to cheapen yourself before you become worthless?

With that in mind, here's a useful business tip that has been worth thousands to me over the years. If you are just starting out in business, don't sell yourself out at £350 a day. Sell yourself out at £1,000 a day. However, offer them an introductory special deal of £350 for the day. When I started off with Independent Thinking, I offered schools an hour-long motivational taster for sixth-form students. It was a good way into schools, many of which are still clients 20 years later. In one school, the head of sixth form told me that the students had decided they didn't think it was worth spending their limited funds on me for an hour. I told him that I would do it for free; however, if, at the end of the session, they felt that it had been worth £50, they should pay me. I left the school with £50 cash and a booking to go back and deliver a full day's INSET at my normal rate.

21 Ways of Knowing You Have Spent Too Long on Twitter

1. You start to think of people who you have never met, who you will never meet, whose face you have never seen and whose real name you will never know, as your 'friends'.

2. You think that the people you follow and who follow you are a cross-section of society and start to believe that all of society is like you. And the people who aren't are just wrong. Or freaks.

3. You like the idea of having 'followers' a little too much.

4. You have a small celebration every time your followers' total goes past a number that ends in a zero.

5. You mistake your number of followers as a reflection of your popularity in the real world.

6. You find your entire weekend is spoiled because someone you have never known has 'unfollowed' you for no reason.

7. Your heart misses a beat every time a complete stranger retweets you.

8. You think tweeting angrily about something to people who share your anger is doing something about it.

9. You think tweeting angrily about something to people who share your anger will change something. Anything.

10. You are starting to blur the distinction between your thoughts and your tweets.

11. You experience something mildly interesting and immediately start putting it into 140 characters in your head.

12. You experience something mildly interesting and stop experiencing it in order to tweet about it.

13. You compose tweets in your head as you go about your daily life, even if you never send them.

14. You start to believe the blurb you put in your profile.

15. You think people under the age of 25 will think you're cool because you're into 'social media'.

16. You think people under the age of 25 actually care about what happens on Twitter.

17. You mistake things that are unimportant with things that are important because they appear in your timeline.

18. You end arguments with a hashtag. In your head.

19. You don't have an opinion until one emerges in your timeline.

20. You see a new photo of yourself and you wonder how it would look scaled down as your new avatar.

21. You're increasingly finding that you're no longer able or willing to concentrate right to the end of any sentence with more than 140 charact

Thunks

If science can't prove something works does it not work even if it works?

If you turn a speaker upside down does the music come out upside down, and is it the same for the light when you turn a torch upside down?

Do flames have sides?

Would an iPod with one track on it work in 'shuffle' mode?

Is 'Toll road clear' on motorway signs a form of advertising, and is it more so the case if the non-toll road is also clear?

Is a dream real?

Does a room weigh more if it has a strong smell in it?

The Conversation Between an Angry Teenager and an Adult

Adult: Your room is a mess. Does nobody do anything around here?

Angry Teenager: I don't want to be a nobody. I want to be a somebody!

Adult: OK. Well, the world is in a mess and somebody needs to do something about it.

Teachers – What Do You Teach?

The answer to the question, of course, is children. You teach children. You might be teaching them maths or science or how to spell or, heaven forefend, the kings and queens of England, but the answer to the question is always the same. You teach children. You teach them about maths or science or how to spell or how to string a list of dates and events together, but you should never lose sight of the 'who' whilst focusing on the 'what'.

But there is a bigger goal. You must teach them to think.

Beyond the goal of teaching children to know things, to pass exams, to get through school, to find a place in the system, we need to teach children to reflect critically on what is going on around them and to ask whether that's the way it should be.

For example, when the Secretary of State for Education in the UK tells us he wants history lessons to 'celebrate the distinguished role of these islands in the history of the world',[1] we need children who can stop, think and start to wonder what it was like for the people on the receiving end of British ambitions in the world. While Britain's role in eradicating the slave trade makes Great Britain a 'beacon of liberty for others to emulate' and the country is celebrating the inge-

---

1   Michael Gove quoted in C. Higgins, 'Historians Say Michael Gove Risks Turning History Lessons into Propaganda Classes', *The Guardian*, 17 August 2011. Available at www.theguardian.com/politics/2011/aug/17/academics-reject-gove-history-lessons (accessed 12 August 2013).

nuity of an engineer like James Watt on the new £50 note, writers like Eduardo Galeano, in his 1973 book *The Open Veins of Latin America*, points out: 'Capital accumulated in the triangular (slave) trade made possible the invention of the steam engine: James Watt was subsidized by businessmen who had made their fortunes in that trade.'[2]

Not to mention the list that appeared in *New Scientist* detailing the '20 deadliest events in human history' in which the British (or more accurately the English) appear in no fewer than six of them.[3]

By bringing these facts to people's attention, the only 'anti' thing I'm being is anti-ignorant. If children want to grow up to be Genghis Khan or Rupert Murdoch or best friends with the Secretary of State for Defence, then there is only so much teachers can do about it. But at least we will have taught them to see the world from different sides, to know that there is always another way, that the louder someone says something is 'fact', the more likely it is that it is simply their opinion.

The great quote from Archbishop Desmond Tutu sums it up in many ways. He once said: 'When the missionaries came to Africa they had the Bible and we had the land. They said, "Let us pray." We closed our eyes. When we opened them we had the Bible and they had the land.' Make it about bankers and the rest of

---

2   E. Galeano, *The Open Veins of Latin America: Five Centuries of the Pillage of a Continent* (London: Serpent's Tail, 2009).

3   'The 20 Worst Things People Have Done to Each Other', *New Scientist*, 21 October 2011. Available at: www.newscientist.com/embedded/20worst (accessed 12 August 2013).

us, and add something about watching *Big Brother* instead of praying, and you have where we are now.

There are student protests going on around the world today as young people start to open their eyes and begin to understand what has happened. Do you talk to your students about them, encourage them to be part of it, to understand the issues, to decide whether to participate or not, and do so as a conscious decision, not one borne out of apathy or ignorance?

The Times Higher Education website posted a fascinating account of Britain's great – but rather hushed up – heritage of student protests and school strikes.[4] What was the response of the authorities then? Merely to dismiss them as rebels, the same response that happens around the world today. After all, according to the November 1889 issue of *The Educational News*,

> *Obedience is the first rule of school life … School strikes are therefore not merely acts of disobedience, but a reversal of the primary purpose of schools … They are manifestations of a serious deterioration in the moral fibre of the rising generation … They will prove dangerous centres of moral contamination.*[5]

If your students went on strike how would you treat them? If you led your students in a protest how would your boss treat you?

---

4   C. Bloom, 'When the Kids are United', *Times Higher Education*, 20 January 2011. Available at: www.timeshighereducation.co.uk/414867.article (accessed 12 August 2013).

5   Quoted in ibid.

So, teach children to open their eyes, to see what is around them, to question, to ask why and why not. Don't teach children *to* the exam. *For* the exam maybe, but not simply to it. Qualifications are an unavoidable evil in the current absence of any other way of assessing children, so cover your back but sleep at night too, as I have said elsewhere. Know that you have done more than just school children, play the game, pass the exam and pass the buck. Open their minds to question, to reflect, to look beneath the surface, to have beliefs that they will fight for and fight for the beliefs of others, even if they don't agree with them.

In other words, what do you teach? I teach children, and I teach them to think for themselves, before it's too late.

155

Observations

Some of the most intelligent people I've ever met have
been some of the worst teachers I've ever had.

The look on a workman's face is the same in any language.

When performing any sort of sport, always be better than your kit.

The opposite of love is deceit.

When Bad Science Leads to Good Practice

The bigger sin in the classroom is not to try new things based on flimsy evidence but the inertia that leads to trying nothing new, ever. Blind persistence in practices that produce inadequate results is a crime against children in the name of education, far more so than simply trying something new to see if it produces better results. After all, without bad science we wouldn't have chemistry, metallurgy, cosmetics, gunpowder, Sir Isaac Newton or Harry Potter. And even snake oil is proving to be effective against arthritis, if you use the right snakes.[1]

157

---

1 'Chinese water-snake oil contains 20 percent eicosapentaenoic acid (EPA), one of the two types of omega-3 fatty acids most readily used by our bodies', according to a November 2007 article by Cynthia Graber in *Scientific American* entitled 'Snake Oil Salesmen Were On To Something'. Available at: www.scientificamerican.com/article.cfm?id=snake-oil-salesmen-knew-something (accessed 12 August 2013).

Standing Still

What you miss by standing still
You see by driving somewhere

What you miss by driving somewhere
You see by riding somewhere

What you miss by riding somewhere
You see by walking somewhere

What you miss by walking somewhere
You see by standing still.

Your One-Minute Three-Step MBA in Crisis Management

When it comes to dealing with a crisis, the best piece of advice I have ever read is as follows:

1. Get the cow out of the ditch.
2. Find out how the cow got into the ditch.
3. Keep the cow from going back into the ditch.[1]

The important bit is doing them in the right order.

1   A. Mulcahy, 'The Best Advice I Ever Got', *Fortune*, 21 March 2005.

The Four Stages of Modern Life

1. You live.
2. You work.
3. You die.
4. You retire.

The Merits of
Not Having a Clue

Someone I know keeps getting promoted, despite her protestations. From being awarded the job in the first place to taking on further leadership responsibilities as she moves closer to the 'the top', her response is always the same: 'But I don't know what to do!'

It seems, though, that the less she knows what to do, the better qualified she is for the job. Not knowing what to do is not the same as being incompetent. Being incompetent is about knowing what to do and doing it badly, or not knowing what to do and doing nothing, or doing the wrong thing more often than doing the right thing, or not knowing that what you are doing is the wrong thing, or knowing it is the wrong thing but hoping you'll get away with it. Not knowing what to do, on the other hand, means to approach a new position in a spirit of honesty and openness, constantly asking the question, 'Is doing this thing the right thing to be doing?'

If you approach a job with a plan, you immediately start to close down the possibilities and miss the opportunities that you didn't know were going to come your way when you took the job. And one man's plan is another man's dogma. Take a look at politics if you don't believe me. 'Elect us and this is what we'll do, regardless,' does not seem to be a grown-up way of running a country. 'These are our values. Elect us and we will stay true to our values and act accordingly as the unforeseen comes our way,' seems like a far more honest approach. If you're going to take a stand, take one on the side of what you believe in, not what you will or won't do.

Of course, such a stance of professional creative ignorance works best if you are in leadership. Different if you are a dentist or work for McDonald's.

The Intelligence of Six

(6 + 6) x 6 ideas:

1. What's the square root of 36?
2. The answer's 6, what's the question?
3. You have two hours to turn this £6 into as big a return as possible ...
4. How would life be different if we worked in base 6 and not base 10?
5. What would you do if you only had 6 years to live? 6 days? 6 minutes?
6. Design a new numerical symbol for '6'.
7. How many things can you make out of the symbol '6'?
8. Write a poem entitled '6'.
9. Get from 'dog' to 'combine harvester' in 6 steps.
10. What are the 6 biggest problems facing the world today?
11. Come up with 6 answers to each.
12. Why is it 6° centigrade?
13. What's the most important thing about 6 a.m.? 6 p.m.?
14. Is a 6 on its side a 6 or a 9?
15. How could you make life better for 6-year-olds?
16. Write a tune with only 6 different notes in it.
17. Design a car for 6 people.
18. Why do insects have 6 legs and not more? Or less?

19. How could you work out if the idea of '6 degrees of separation' is really true?

20. Who are the 6 people who mean the most to you?

21. Who are the 6 people you mean the most to?

22. Prepare a three-course meal with only 6 ingredients.

23. Make someone laugh in only 6 words.

24. Tell me the story of Cinderella in only 6 words.

25. Tell me your life story in only 6 words. 6 pictures.

26. Come up with 6 uses for a fork.

27. There is an Amazonian tribe who only work in 2s – how would you get across the concept of '6' to them?

28. What are the 6 most important lessons every 12-year-old should know?

29. You need to find £6 in 6 hours – what 6 things could you do?

30. Which are the 6 most important species on the planet and why?

31. You are marooned for 6 days on the moors – what are the first 6 things you would do?

32. There has been an accident in a tunnel and you have to put a 6-person rescue team together – who would you choose and why?

33. Attacking aliens have asked for 6 people to represent planet earth – who should we send?

34. Get from the word 'dog' to 'cat' in 6 steps.

35. Find the word for '6' in 6 different languages.

36. Find the symbol for '6' in 6 different scripts.

37. Get from 6 to 666 in 6 steps.

38. What 6 things would happen if there were suddenly no 6s in the world?

39. Name 6 things that make you happy.

40. Name 6 things that would make someone else happy.

41. You are the head of a school – what are the 6 biggest challenges you face? What are the 6 smallest?

42. Name 6 things you could do today to make the world a better place.

43. What 6 things could you do to fix a dripping tap?

44. Name 6 emotions you feel when watching a football match.

45. Name 6 emotions you feel during a science lesson.

46. Name 6 causes of a headache.

47. Name 'The Nation's 6 Favourite 6-Letter Words' in your opinion and why.

48. Name 6 things you could do to halt climate change.

49. Name 6 things you want to do before you die.

50. Name the 6 most important people in the history of the world and why.

51. Name the 6 most important inventions in the history of the world and why.

52. You have to pack a suitcase for a 6-week holiday in Australia and you're only allowed 6 items – what would you take?

53. Name 6 reasons why 6 is a special number.

54. Write a 6-word slogan to sell yourself to a potential employer.

55. Name 6 things you'd save if your house was on fire. What if it was your school on fire?

56. Name 6 steps to a healthier lifestyle.

57. What are the 6 longest words you know?

58. Name 6 technological inventions you would come up with if you were Bill Gates.

59. If you typed '6' into Google, what do you think would be the first 6 things that would come up?

60. What are the 6 most important companies in the world today?

61. Name 6 uses for old people.

62. Name 6 ways to reduce traffic congestion where you live.

63. Name 6 reasons why your car won't start.

64. What 6 things could you do if your computer is running slow?

65. You've got 6 people coming to dinner and a budget of £6 per person – what would you prepare for them? What if your budget was just £6 in total?

66. You have a pen, some paper, a mobile phone, a spoon and a computer connected to the Internet – name 6 ways you could make money just using that equipment.

67. Design a 6-room house for a family of 6.

68. Identify 6 ways to reduce teenage crime.

69. Identify 6 ways to reduce teenage pregnancy.

70. What are the 6 worst things you could say to a friend? The 6 best?

71. Name 6 things with 6 sides.

72. Name 6 things a horse needs.

Observations

Sometimes, it's only when the fog clears that you can see the maze you're in.

You can tell a friend by their actions and a true friend by their reactions.

Be the media you want to see in the world.

Out of ten press-ups, the ninth is always the hardest.

The Game of Solitaire

It is important to understand the differences between the following terms:

Alone

On your own

Lonely

The first is a choice.

The second is a sign of resilience and self-determination.

The third leads to wretchedness.

Will Smith and the Flower Paradox

A teacher friend told me recently of a school photography trip she was leading where the group had been meeting outside the famous Peninsula Hotel in Hong Kong. One girl was so busy with her assignment, photographing a flower outside the building, that she missed the American A-lister Will Smith walk right past her.

Is that:

1. A good thing because we should be teaching young people to focus on the beauty in the natural world and ignore the shallow distraction of fame and celebrity.
2. A bad thing because we are so intent on teaching children to do what they are told, and learn what we set them in advance, that they end up missing unexpected once-in-a-lifetime opportunities when they present themselves.
3. All of the above.

Trying To Be a
Good Man

Above the M5,
On a bridge, a dog barks at
Cars. The sun still shines.

Observations

It is so annoying when people interrupt you with what they're thinking when you're trying to have a decent monologue with them.

I went to buy a pocket and they said, 'What size do you want?'

In Suffolk, where there's more sky than people, if you drive slowly enough you will eventually get stuck behind something.

It would be helpful if the sign at the entrance to every cemetery in the land read 'All human life is here'.

Train Your Dog Like a Child

1. A dog is for life, not just for Christmas.
2. Be consistent.
3. Catch him in, don't just catch him out – reward good behaviour more than you punish poor behaviour.
4. Let the dog know he is doing wrong *when* he is doing wrong.
5. He really does want to please you.
6. Make sure that he knows the basic rules early on.
7. His behaviour is your responsibility.
8. Make sure you offer him huge quantities of encouragement.
9. Ensure you play with him regularly and make work play.
10. Enjoy being with him and make sure he knows it.

Train Your Child Like a Dog

1. A child is for life, not just for Christmas.
2. Be consistent.
3. Catch her in, don't just catch her out – reward good behaviour more than you punish poor behaviour.
4. Let the child know she is doing wrong *when* she is doing wrong.
5. She really does want to please you.
6. Make sure that she knows the basic rules early on.
7. Her behaviour is your responsibility.
8. Make sure you offer her huge quantities of encouragement.
9. Ensure you play with her regularly and make work play.
10. Enjoy being with her and make sure she knows it.

Observations

To identify your desired school ethos, establish what you want society to look like in 30 years and work backwards from there.

The only way to remain in control when you are descending a muddy bank is not to edge down carefully but to run down as fast as you can. So it is with all slippery slopes.

In all the student demonstrations that have taken place in the last 100 years, governments should be fearful of the fact the young people are on the streets not because they have been educated but because they have not been educated enough. They are fighting for, and not as a result of, their education.

In the short term rock beats water. But only in the short term.

There's No Such Thing as an Educational Expert

I have been called many things in my time but the one I am increasingly uncomfortable with is the title of 'educational expert'. The more I reflect on what I know about education, the more I realise that it is a tiny fraction of what this thing called 'education' is all about. Who am I to claim to tell you about your job? I don't know you, your children or your environment in anywhere near enough detail to be able to say with any authority, 'Try this and it will work'.

When I work with teachers I may well suggest ideas for them to try that I feel, based on previous experience, have a good probability of working. If they get back to me only to tell me that the idea didn't work, my response is to ask them, politely, how they managed to get that idea not to work. There's no such thing as bad feedback after all.

That said, I am increasingly of a mind that anyone standing before a group of educational professionals and proclaiming in all confidence, 'This works' is actually saying, in all frankness, 'This worked'. Rather than saying 'Do this!' I suggest that 'Try this!' is a more honest imperative, although 'Adapt this!' beats them both hands down.

Dutch education professor Knud Illeris writes that learning, something he sets apart from simply maturing as a human being which happens naturally, involves the interplay of three dimensions:

1. What we are learning.
2. Why we need to learn it.
3. How this process interacts with the environment around us and the people in that environment.[1]

In a classroom setting, that makes for a great many variables at play which will determine what will work and what won't at any given time. As any teacher will tell you, the lesson that goes so well with one group will fall flat on its face in the next lesson with a different group or even the following day with the same group.

Furthermore, what isn't explicit in Illeris' model is the role that the teacher plays in the success or otherwise of the learning. Emotions are contagious and what the teacher brings to the lesson can make or break that lesson, regardless of much else.

So, how can anyone claim to be an expert when there are so many variables at play, changing on an almost minute-by-minute basis? While I have always advocated that a classroom is a laboratory and teachers should always experiment with their lessons – doing things with children and not to them – they do not

---

1   K. Illeris, *How We Learn: Learning and Non-Learning in School and Beyond* (London: Routledge, 2007).

function under laboratory conditions, so any claim to be able to assess educational practices with pharmaceutical-like accuracy and assiduity should be treated with care. Much as you should do with pharmaceutical research anyway.

The role of the 'educational expert', then, isn't so much one of sharing answers and distributing truths but of posing questions. What marks an expert is his or her ability to know (a) which questions to put to a group of teachers or school leaders and (b) how to pose the question. That's it.

Mind you, the one thing worse than an expert telling you this is how it should be in education is a politician doing it.

30 Things That Exams Don't Measure

1. Self-esteem
2. Confidence
3. Fairness
4. Creativity
5. Resilience
6. Sense of humour
7. Sense of perspective
8. Ability to be with others
9. Ability to be with yourself
10. Mindfulness
11. Self-control
12. Self-awareness
13. Sense of justice
14. Sense of injustice
15. Moral code
16. Motivation to do well
17. Motivation to keep on learning
18. Motivation to contribute
19. Curiosity
20. Gumption
21. Resourcefulness
22. Ingenuity
23. Ability to love
24. Ability to be loved
25. Ethics
26. Emotional intelligence
27. Empathy
28. Ability to make people laugh
29. Ability to make people cry
30. Ability to train a kestrel

The Space Between the Stars

When you look at the night sky and you see stars you, of course, see patterns in the stars. It's like trying to find a meaning in your life. If you look long enough and join up the random elements, you'll find one. For millennia, humans have looked at the stars and made of them animals and symbols and gods, like some great celestial dot-to-dot puzzle.

Or at least that's what I thought until I went stargazing in Chile.

Here, I learned that when the Aztecs looked to the heavens they too saw animals (a lot of llamas). However, they didn't see animals in the patterns of the stars but in the space between the stars. I had never thought about the space between the stars before. I had been too busy looking at what was there to even notice what wasn't there. And in those spaces to find a new beauty and a new way of seeing.

Trust

When it comes to business relationships I don't do contracts. Instead I have one rule:

Trust everyone once.

It hasn't let me down yet, although sometimes you have to trust certain people like you would a net curtain. You can see through them but you hope no one else can.

And whenever I meet a new associate or business partner for the first time, I always end the conversation with the following line:

You can't upset me.[1]

If it's business then, by definition, it's not personal. If a colleague is unhappy they should tell me so and I can do something about it, even if it's just to explain to them why nothing will change. If they keep their issues to themselves, there is no hope of anything being resolved and the relationship will soon sour.

I will also lose faith in you if you take more than you give.

---

1   That said, it is not entirely true. You can upset me. Lie to me.

Why Am I Here?

Why am I here? History lesson.

Why *am* I here? Philosophy lesson.

Why am *I* here? Science lesson.

Why am I *here?* Geography lesson.

Why am I hear? Literacy lesson.

The Money-Back Guarantee

lways, always offer a money-back guarantee. It's something called 'risk reversal'. Buying any new product or service is a risk. A money-back guarantee means it's your risk and not theirs.

And make it unequivocal too. One school (only once) said that what I had delivered was not as good as they had hoped. We wrote back and apologised and told them they had no need to pay for my time or expenses. They wrote back saying it wasn't that bad and sent me a cheque for half the full fee. I sent it back. They sent it back. I stuck it on my office wall. It's still there.

Thunks

Is handing your criminal child over to the police a greater act of love than not doing so?

Can you not yet have heard your second favourite ever song?

Does the Church need the poor?

Can you have the last word by remaining silent?

Do you have the same number of thoughts each day?

Is it undemocratic to be made to vote?

Is taking a £1 coin more like stealing than taking something that cost £1?

Can everybody wear exclusive clothes?

Three Questions to Ask Before Every Training Day

1. Are you as good as you can be?

    No one will say that they have nothing to learn, yet too many act that way. It should be remembered also that there is a clear distinction between learning something new and doing something different. The former is pointless without being hotly pursued by the latter.[1]

2. Are we as good as each other?

    I see no reason why you can't at least attempt to be as good as the person next door. I was amazed when I heard for the first time the line about there being 'bigger in-school variation than between-school variation'. This is the same in Singapore as it is in England. Don't go on a course till you've spent an hour next door.

---

1   Sometimes they come in a different order but so be it.

3. Is what you do going to make a difference to the future?

    It is clear that your actions will have an effect on your children. For better or for worse. The bigger question, though, is whether your actions will help them become something that will, in due course, have a positive effect on the world. If all you are doing for them is to teach them to pass exams then maybe the answer is no.

Three Responses That Are Worse Than Saying No

'Let's be practical.'

'Perhaps some other time.'

'Yes, but …'

Observations

Love is something you give. Happiness is something you take.

Politics is the art of knowing which lies to share and which facts to conceal.

Whereas most people confuse the difficult for the impossible,
a special few simply don't know the difference.

The Mirror

I met a man
Whom I believed
To be a liar
So he was.

Things to Watch Out For When You See the Word 'Independent'

Don't mistake 'independent' for impartial.

Don't mistake 'independent' for unbiased.

Don't mistake 'independent' for neutral.

Don't mistake 'independent' for factual.

Don't mistake 'independent' for the truth, especially when their truth matches yours.

N.B. If the word 'independent' is followed by the term 'think tank' then the above holds doubly true.

Thunks

Should we teach our children not to believe what they read, trust what they hear or do what they're told?

If you shine a candle in a mirror do you get twice as much light?

Does a window have a front and a back?

Would you eat in a restaurant which advertised that it used only the best cockroach traps?

Does a digital photograph of a black sheet of paper use fewer megabytes of space than a digital photo of a white sheet of paper?

Are the bubbles in the bottle before you open it?

Does your dog know what it did last summer?

Larks Ascending

When it comes to singing, the male skylark proves its sexual and physical superiority by staying the highest for the longest period of time.

In Dubai, Hong Kong, London, Santiago and elsewhere, towers designed to be the highest for the longest period of time have all been built by men.

Coincidence?

Captain Pouch College

Not far from where I grew up in middle England is a college named after a famous land-owning family from the area, the Treshams. This is the family responsible for the curious 16th century triangular lodge you see from the train as you head north about an hour out of London's St Pancras station. In the same town there used to be a school named after the Montagu family, another one of the area's big land-owning families.

There are also many enclosed fields.

In the early 1600s the Treshams were having a spot of bother. They, like many other wealthy land-owning families with institutions named after them, were helping themselves to what had been common grazing land. Land that had not belonged to anyone in particular and had been used by the common people to raise their livestock, grow crops and feed their families was being enclosed to keep the commoners out and the livestock of the wealthy families in. With similar acts of public robbery taking place across the country, a growing sense of outrage increasingly took the form of what these days we call 'direct action', namely 'digging' and 'levelling' the various fences, hedges and ditches that had been constructed illegally.

In 1607, this was taking place across the Midlands, especially in Warwickshire, Leicestershire and the Montagu's and Tresham's home turf of Northamptonshire. In the words of the Diggers of Warwickshire:

> *Wee, as members of the whole, doe feele the smarte of these incroaching Tirants, which would grind our flesh upon the whetstone of poverty, and make our loyall hearts to faint with breathing, so that they may dwell by themselves in the midst of theyr heards of fatt weathers.*[1]

In May of that year, around 1,000 peasant men, women and children gathered to 'level' the enclosures the Treshams had constructed in and around Rockingham Forest. The rebel leader was a mysterious figure called John Reynolds, who went by the Jacobean superhero name of Captain Pouch. He was a local tinker who claimed to have divine backing and that the pouch he carried with him contained 'that which shall keep you from all harm'. He also urged his followers to refrain from using violence against the landowners.

As far as the King James I was concerned, such gatherings were purely and simply criminal acts in which 'some of the meaner sort of our people did of late assemble themselves in riotous and tumultuous maner'. Despite Montagu twice reading the King's proclamation, from which that description comes, the

---

1 Quoted at www.newtonrebels.org.uk/rebels/history.htm (accessed 28 August 2013).

rebels refused to disperse. A massacre ensued with 40 or so of the peasants killed, many taken prisoner and held in a nearby church and the leaders hanged, drawn and quartered, and their remains displayed in towns across the county in an exemplary manner.

All this took place over 450 years ago and only a few miles away from where I grew up and went to school, where I was taught stealing was wrong and that I should respect my betters, yet I knew nothing of the Midland Revolt of 1607 until very recently (a serendipitous discovery involving a new iPad, a Kindle app, the Guttenberg Project, Marx and Engels' *Communist Manifesto* and Wikipedia). The wealthy families whose land and impressive properties I grew up amongst had actually been thieves, stealing from ordinary people, leaving them no choice but to starve or to rise up and take direct action. Yet 450 years later, it was these thieves who were having the schools and colleges named after them with barely a trace of the victims.

Maybe every conversation with the land-owning classes should begin with, 'And pray, tell me, how did you acquire your land in the first place?'

What the uprising did achieve was focus attention on the actions of the Tresham family who were held to account by parliament but whose punishment amounted to little more than a small tax on their new ill-gotten land. They got to keep the land. The family fell into decline not long after the revolt, a fate linked more to Francis Tresham's involvement in the Gunpowder Plot than the family's treatment of the common people. Most of their land was acquired by the Montagu family who, through marriage, went on to become the Dukes of Buccleuch, who are among the country's biggest landowners.

Perhaps more of a lesson to the followers of John Reynolds than his public torture and gruesome death was the fact that his pouch turned out to contain nothing other than green cheese.

In other news …

In August 2011, riots spread across a number of major cities in England. In an address to the House of Commons, reported in Hansard, Prime Minister David Cameron, a descendent of King William IV, said of the disturbances: 'It is criminality, pure and simple – and there is absolutely no excuse for it.'[2]

In an article in *The Guardian*,[3] one observer of the riots in London described them as 'inevitable', explaining the thinking behind what happened: 'Right, you ain't got no money, I ain't got no money, we ain't got nowhere to go, no one gives a crap about us, so why are we sitting here trying to be decent people when that's not getting us nowhere?'[4]

In the same Hansard report, the Prime Minister responded to calls by Conservative MPs for 'stiff sentences' for the rioters by saying: 'it is perfectly possible

---

2   Hansard, HC (series 5), vol. 531, col. 1051 (11 August 2011).

3   *The Guardian* was originally known as the *Manchester Guardian*. It replaced the *Manchester Observer*, a publication set up to support the voice of public protest following the Peterloo Massacre in 1819.

4   T. Newburn, P. Lewis, E. Addley and M. Taylor, 'David Cameron, the Queen and the Rioters' Sense of Injustice', *The Guardian*, 5 December 2011. Available at: www.theguardian.com/uk/2011/dec/05/cameron-queen-injustice-english-rioters (accessed 12 August 2013).

for courts to set some exemplary sentences, to send out a clear message, and I for one hope they will do just that.'[5]

By August 2012, a total of 1,292 rioters had been handed custodial sentences totalling 1,800 years, an average of 16.8 months. This was four times higher than the normal tariff for public order offences.

A report in the *Daily Telegraph* described how 21-year-old Anderson Fernandes from Manchester was jailed for 16 months for helping himself to an ice cream during the disturbances, taking two licks then giving it away.[6]

A few years before the riots, the *Telegraph* had also broken the story of the MPs' expenses scandal. By February 2010, 344 MPs had given back a total of £985,129.52. A handful went to prison.

A few years before that, at the request of the then Prime Minister Tony Blair, the owner of the *Daily Telegraph* was awarded a life peerage and the Elizabethan superhero name of Baron Black. However, in 2007, a Chicago court found Black guilty of embezzlement to the tune of many millions of dollars.

---

5   Hansard, HC (series 5), vol. 531, col. 1090 (11 August 2011).

6   'UK Riots: Looter Who Pinched Too [*sic*] Scoops of Ice-Cream Jailed for 16 Months', *Daily Telegraph*, 26 August 2011. Available at: www.telegraph.co.uk/news/uknews/law-and-order/8722733/UK-riots-Looter-who-pinched-too-scoops-of-ice-cream-jailed-for-16-months.html (accessed 12 August 2013). Also appearing in court that day, according to the report, was a man 'so drunk he forgot he'd been in a riot'.

Entirely coincidentally, Conrad Black's father's name was George Montegu Black. Montagu School has now been given to an academy chain. No longer named after the Montagu family, it carries the Buccleuch family name.

There is no school or college named after Captain Pouch. But there is a beer.

Observations

I'm sure the Co-op does a great funeral but somehow I don't want to be buried with the same typeface as my shopping.

When it comes to injustice we need to encourage young people not to have an opinion but to have a reaction. Then to have an opinion.

You can't follow the crowd and lead the field at the same time.

I once raced my daughter to touch a lighthouse. I think we all should touch a lighthouse once in our lives.

My Chilean Education

For a period of 18 months, I lived and worked in Santiago, Chile. For most people in the West, Chile doesn't really enter the radar unless it's about pulling miners out of the ground or working out which is the best value Cabernet Sauvignon to choose.

However, Chile's role as a guinea pig[1] in the neo-liberal, free-market world order we are currently, er, enjoying means that we should all give this wonderful country some thought.

In a community that is still divided by a common history, where the poor stay poor, helping the rich get richer, here are some of the lessons I learned, the importance of which echo way beyond Chile's national boundaries.

1. Living with integrity is, without fail, the hardest option.

2. For every attempted reaction there is an equal and negative action – the rule of status quo.

3. The rich have the poor stitched up.

4. To achieve power you promise change but to retain it you busily change nothing.

---

1   Although 'laboratory rat' may be a more accurate term given the levels of violence and coercion involved. For more on this read Naomi Klein's *The Shock Doctrine: The Rise of Disaster Capitalism* (London: Penguin, 2007).

5. Having hope makes life almost unbearable yet, when life is absolutely unbearable, hope is the only thing that sustains you.

6. The world has been moulded by rich white men for rich white men.

7. A developing country that persists in only appointing friends at the expense of talent is not a developing country.

8. 99% of people are born with 1% of the power to change the world; 1% of the people are born with 99% of the power to ensure the world stays the same.

9. To say, 'Let's be practical' is another way of saying, 'Let nothing change'.

10. To foil a revolution, smile, say yes, do nothing.

11. Those who talk most of their principles exhibit them least.

12. When it comes to charity, it is easier to give when you have nothing to lose.

13. No matter how rich you are, it seems you can't buy guilt.

14. Having political parties on the centre-left and the centre-right guarantees the complete equilibrium of the entire system.

15. Reconciliation is impossible without justice.

16. The levels of activity exerted in order to achieve power are then matched by similar levels of inactivity in order to retain it.

17. A dictator's enemies do not last long but his friends survive indefinitely.

18. Not voting is a political act.

19. With charity, a signed cheque wipes the slate clean.

20. If it wasn't for the poor, religion could actually be used for good.

21. Although out of the reach of many, the will of God is not that expensive to purchase.

22. To be able to say, 'It wasn't me – it was God', makes attending all those expensive Sunday masses worthwhile.

23. Education is the process by which we teach the majority of children that this is the way it is whilst teaching the minority how to ensure this is the way it stays.

24. The rich need the poor in order to stay rich.

25. Failing to educate children in morals is failing to educate them.

26. The statue of the Virgin Mary on San Cristóbal Hill looking out over Santiago has her back to the rich people for a reason.

27. Ensuring nothing changes is a full-time job.

28. When you are powerful enough, even you don't have to believe the lies you tell to explain your corruption.

29. Your failings are always the result of someone else's.

30. Doing something is far more important than achieving anything.

31. Telling the truth is too cheap for rich people to bother with.

32. Alcohol, shopping and television are the means by which we hide from ourselves how imperfect democracy is.

33. The more experts there are, the less expertise there is.

34. Charity is icing a rotting cake.

35. To maintain power you must ensure the buck never stops.

36. Academics love new ideas and very old ones. They soon become bored with current, useful ones.

37. It takes a great deal of effort to do nothing.

38. For charity to work it needs people who are too ill or too poor to say no.

39. Nothing is so dehumanising or dangerous to the environment as the word 'resource'.

40. The ruling classes own history.

41. Twitter is the 21st century's revolutionary pamphlet. This is not 100% a good thing.

42. Like grease and dust, the right and the left stick together when faced with a clean-up.

43. The further down the pile you are, the higher up you attach the blame.

44. A job is the knife your boss holds at your throat.

45. Everyone is an expert on education, except teachers.

46. No matter how many life sentences someone may be serving for torture and murder, there will always be some people ready to throw him a party.

47. Beggars have the same right to strike as the rest of us.

48. The less you steal, the greater the punishment.

49. The more authority you have to say no, the less power you have to say yes.

50. People deserve that which they are not prepared to do anything to change.

51. Many people live in poverty exhibiting a dignity that poverty doesn't deserve.

52. Never, ever, appoint anyone you fear may be more intelligent than you are.

53. Being poor is free but staying that way costs a lot of money.

54. The worst kind of exam system is one designed to find out what children don't know.

55. Being at the top of the bottom of the heap is still the bottom of the heap.

56. The more powerful you think you are, the quicker you are not to answer your e-mails.

57. The difference between latchkey kids and kids with maids is that the rich children get to watch their own TVs after school.

58. Street dogs have better lives than pet dogs; pet dogs have better lives than street children.

59. Neo-liberalism means never having to say you're sorry.

60. Like water to the sea, money will always work its way to the rich.

61. The opposite of poverty is dignity.

62. Father Alberto Hurtado's funeral socks have a better life than most of the people he tried to help.

On Leadership II

When you're a leader:

1. If you want respect, you give respect.
2. If you want loyalty, you give opportunity.
3. If you want obedience, you're not a leader.

Crowd to Brian:
'Yes, We're All Individuals'

These are my two contradictory philosophies of life:

Do unto others as you would have them do unto you[1]

and

I do not recognise anyone's right to one minute of my life. Nor to any part of my energy. Nor to any achievement of mine.[2]

They are reconciled in the words of classical musician Daniel Barenboim:

Each note must be aware of its own boundaries. The same rules that apply to individuals in society apply to notes in music as well ... It is necessary for the human being to contribute to society in a very individual way; this makes the whole much larger than the sum of its parts. Individuality and collectivism

---

1   Attributed to the Bible but also found 'in some form in almost every ethical tradition', according to philosopher Simon Blackburn. See S. Blackburn, *Ethics: A Very Short Introduction* (Oxford: Oxford University Press, 2001).

2   From Howard Roark's famous courtroom speech in Ayn Rand's *The Fountainhead* (London: Penguin Classics, 2007 [1943]).

need not be mutually exclusive; in fact, together they are capable of enhancing human existence.[3]

By striving to be yourself, and only yourself, you make the world and everyone in it all the richer for it.

3   D. Barenboim, *Everything is Connected: The Power of Music* (London: Orion, 2008).

Advice II

Never move from. Always move towards. Life is like a dog. If it sees you running away it hunts you down. The only time you should move back is to take a better run up as you move forward.

Observations

Learning about environmental issues by going to a theme park
is like going to Disneyland to learn about mice.

Books are written by people too lazy to write the aphorisms read by people
too lazy to read books.

Are you old enough to remember a time when the only people you could
speak to were those in the same room as you?

In Santiago, silence is the sound of just one dog barking.

One person can change the world, they just can't do it alone.